The Wicked Queen

Translated by Julie Rose

The Wicked Queen

*The Origins of
the Myth of
Marie-Antoinette*

Chantal Thomas

ZONE BOOKS · NEW YORK

1999

The publisher would like to thank the French Ministry of
Culture for its assistance with this translation.

© 1999 Urzone, Inc.
611 Broadway, Suite 608
New York, NY 10012

Originally published in France as *La Reine scélérate:
Marie-Antoinette dans les pamphlets* © 1989 Editions du Seuil.

Printed in the United States of America.

Distributed by The MIT Press,
Cambridge, Massachusetts, and London, England

Library of Congress Cataloging-in-Publication Data

Thomas, Chantal.
    [La Reine scélérate. English]
    The wicked queen : the origins of the myth of Marie-
Antoinette / by Chantal Thomas : translated by Julie Rose.
        p.   cm.
    Includes bibliographical references and index.
    ISBN 1-942299-39-6 (cloth). 1. Marie-Antoinette,
Queen, consort of Louis XVI, King of France. 2. France —
History— Revolution, 1789–1799— Pamphlets. 3. Queens —
France — Biography.
    I. Title.
DC137.1.T5613   1997
944'.035'092 — dc21   96-50157
                                                    CIP

Contents

Myth is a type of speech chosen by history:
it cannot possibly evolve from the "nature" of things.
— Roland Barthes, *Mythologies*

Their furious momentum is checked when contemplating their Enemy, the Other, the Foreign Woman — the woman who has all the luck! (October 5, 1789)

Introduction

From a History of Libertinage to the Sudden Rise of a Persona: The Marie-Antoinette of the Pamphlets

When I began in 1987 to become interested in the pamphlets attacking Queen Marie-Antoinette, I saw the research as a third and final part in a history of eighteenth-century libertinage. My essays on the Marquis de Sade had analyzed its systematic, closed, tragic, and transgressive form.[1] A book on the celebrated Venetian adventurer Giacomo Casanova had provided the errant, devil-may-care version.[2] In looking into the pamphlet literature, which, as it approached the revolutionary years, increasingly wallowed in a vulgar representation of aristocratic debauchery even while denouncing it, I wanted to delineate the end of a philosophy and a practice of pleasure indissociable from conditions of existence conducive to idleness and sophistication. Such a philosophy was effectively based on a complete separation of the family values of genealogical and moral continuity and the egotistical values of carnal pleasures, which, far from concerning themselves with enlistment in a lasting relationship, are satisfied with the passing agreement of a complicity. But the more pamphlets I read, as I went between the Bibliothèque Nationale and the Bibliothèque Historique de la Ville de Paris, the more I was convinced that the history of libertinage ended with the French Revolution.[3] In particular, I became more and more amazed and fascinated by the awesome monstrosity of the Marie-Antoinette portrayed in the pamphlets, by her flagrant unreality, and I realized that this would become the object of my research. What was being constructed here, in these brief, repetitive, tirelessly slanderous opuscules, was a caricatured double who lived her own life and developed according to the internal logic of a genre that required "ever worse" as a law of necessity. As Robert Darnton has shown, pamphlet production was a commercial enterprise.[4] Contrary to high literature, it above all obeyed mercantile objectives. Like the tabloid press, its register was hyperbole, excess its motto. The diabolical vocation of Marie-Antoinette was to overstep all the limits, to always outdo herself in frivolousness, indecency, denaturation, scorn for her husband and squandering of the realm, sexual audacity, and murderous lunacy. As a pamphlet heroine, Marie-Antoinette was a woman whose capacity for evil exceeded, by a long shot, all bounds of plausibility.

I threw myself into reading the numerous biographies published on the queen. Whether written in sympathy or with critical detachment, none avoid the flood of lampoons of which the queen was the object. But all concern themselves with the pamphlets as though they had *a direct relationship* with the personality of Louis XVI's wife. Marie-Antoinette's biographers see in these pamphlets either outrageous slander or just deserts, the immediate sanction of a public shocked by Marie-Antoinette's behavior. Works more specifically centered on the pamphlets against Marie-Antoinette, such as Henri d'Almeras's *Les Amoureux de la reine, Marie-Antoinette et les pamphlets royalistes et révolutionnaires* (1907) and Hector Fleischmann's *Les Pamphlets libertins contre Marie-Antoinette* (1907),[5] differ from each other according to their favorable or hostile stance toward the queen, but basically offer the same reading: they are attempts to link the heroine of the pamphlets to the "real" Marie-Antoinette. Both camps judge Marie-Antoinette in terms of the verisimilitude they accord the lampoons. D'Almeras represents the voice for the defense, Fleischmann that for the prosecution. D'Almeras strives to exonerate Marie-Antoinette, to clear her of the crimes the pamphlets impute to her. He reduces alleged evil deeds to careless mistakes made in all innocence. Fleischmann, meanwhile, constructs his book as a terrible arraignment, striving to define the relationship between the queen's behavior and pamphlet propaganda as one of exact correspondence between cause and effect.

Fleischmann makes no secret of his role as inquisitorial judge, nor does he conceal the misogynist prejudices aligning him with the pamphlets. He alerts us at the very beginning of his book: "Flighty, that is the sole excuse offered by the historians. It is also the excuse admitted every day in our courts of law for women who commit adultery. It is the cause of this flightiness — let us maintain the euphemism — which we will investigate here." The case is lost from the start: Marie-Antoinette reveals, to an extraordinary extent, the hatred and fear engendered by the "dark continent" of the feminine. Marie-Antoinette's crime lies not in an act but in a quality of being. Fleischmann appoints himself heir to the judgment of the scandal sheets and the revolutionary Tribunal by decreeing the unbearable lightness of the Queen. She remained frivolous to the bitter end: newspapers at the time reported that despite having her hands tied behind her back, she "sprang lightly," without any help, from the cart carrying her to the guillotine (Marie-Antoinette's agility is equivalent to Mme Roland's smile, parading her intellectual arrogance to the last).

"Frivolous, flighty, reckless — mere faults in a middle-class woman, a crime for a queen — she believed she was on stage, performing before the spectacle of her pleasure. 'I need to be hissed or applauded,' she would say. And they hissed while they waited to guillotine her." Fleischmann's ostensibly virtuous, compensatory, but secretly voyeuristic study presents us with a body of libertine pamphlets against the queen as though they were so many bills of indictment, seeking to demonstrate the logic of a progression in which "this royal head was ripe for contempt before being ripe for the blade." The extent to which the innovation of a mechanical death unleashed metaphors evoking nature and rural life, images of ripe fruit and mown wheat, is strange indeed.

Fleischmann's attitude, which happens to be the most prevalent among historians of the queen, implies a manifold and deliberate use of confusion. Confusion first of all by way of a retroactive illusion, Marie-Antoinette was guillotined: therefore, the crimes of debauchery denounced in the pamphlets must have led her to the guillotine. Such crimes call for the death penalty. Marie-Antoinette was guilty, because she was condemned. In another of his works, *Le Cénacle libertin de Mlle Raucourt* (1912), Fleischmann attempts to rank Marie-Antoinette among the female lovers of the actress who was as famous for her acting talent as for her feminine conquests. He declares: "It would never be futile to show how eighteenth-century society paved the way for the turmoil of the Revolution and what great authenticity it lent to the arguments of the 'reign of virtue' in the Year II."[6] In Fleischmann's eyes, clouded by the sanction of the Revolution, the debauched queen brought on this turmoil and its purificatory violence. According to this retrospective reading, Marie-Antoinette's whole life, as inferred from the pamphlets, unfolds in the shadow of the scaffold that awaits her, as yet invisible but already in place, ready to chasten the Flighty Woman. Clearly the entire "feminine race" is under attack in the queen, as if to say: Stop being so flighty, Women, slow down and be serious!

The sharp angles of a scaffold stand out against the rose bushes of the Petit Trianon. It would have been wiser to locate them in time. To redress people's behavior in the funereal light of what has happened takes no account of the contingency forming the real basis of our decisions, the vital element sanctioning our wildest hopes. In fact, a few weeks before Marie-Antoinette was sentenced, Axel, Count of Fersen, who dreamed of reestablishing royalty in France, proposed to her a list of names for the constitution of a regency government.

The reading exemplified by Fleischmann combines the illusion of retroactivity with an essentialist illusion confusing Nature and History. Any reading that credits the caricature of the pamphlets with a modicum of reality falls into the same confusion. In other words, it remains blind to all that which concerns myth.

Toward an Historical Mythology:
The Teaching of Roland Barthes

A student in a seminar of Roland Barthes, I took *Mythologies* (1957) as a model of inspiration. Barthes was for me much more than a thesis supervisor. He was a friendly guide along the path of a literary criticism, equally devoted to the passion of writing and that of deciphering, equally subject to the twin demands of style and lucidity. The interpretive scouring and demystification at work in *Mythologies* provided me with a guiding principle for approaching the pamphlet literature not as testimony but as an autonomous system endowed with its own rules, its own rhetoric, its particular function — a system which, naturally, was not invented for Marie-Antoinette, but which was rife for centuries and closed in on her from the moment she appeared on the Versailles stage.[7] As a vulnerable target of calumny, Marie-Antoinette merely took over from Mme du Barry, King Louis XV's last favorite. A telling anecdote here: Louis XV employed Beaumarchais, whose life, like his theater, constitutes an inexhaustible mine of roles and adventures, to seek out and destroy the pamphlets written against the king's favorite. When Louis XV died on May 10, 1774, Beaumarchais was in no danger of losing his job. He was to continue under Louis XVI to track down the lampoonists, who were now attacking the young sovereign!

Philippe Roger correctly insists that the definition of myth undergoes certain fluctuations in the work of Barthes and that it ultimately "remains without a stable theoretical status."[8] This instability is evident in Barthes' 1957 postface, "Myth Today," appended to the short texts of *Mythologies* as a scientific justification. His appeal to two dominant sources — the linguistics of Ferdinand de Saussure and the work of Karl Marx — no longer convinces us today and even creates confusion. This rigid application of dogmas or schemas borrowed from other thinkers, this voluntarist transfer, is what has aged in the work of Barthes. It is what ages in any work. What does not age but, on the contrary, continues to enrich us as a vital source that deepens and strengthens any personal discourse, is the active intention manifest in *Mythologies*, the power of freedom and rejection introduced into reading by the twin refusals on which Barthes' approach is based:

1. To consider myth not as an object but as a speech act: "What must be firmly established at the start is that myth is a system of communication, that it is a message. This allows one to perceive that myth cannot possibly be an object, a concept, or an idea; it is a mode of signification, a form. [...] Myth is not defined by the object of its message, but by the way in which it utters this message."[9] Anyone, anything can be mythologized, can become the prey of mythical speech. For me, going from Mme du Barry to Marie-Antoinette within the continuity of pamphlet production is certainly going from one prey to another.

2. To reject all natural evidence from mythologizing speech, to expose it as a deforming and simplifying power. The object,

the person who has become the prey of a mythic speech act, joins in the eternity of essences, whether benign or malignant. Mythic speech no longer belongs to the relative, changing space of human and economic relationships. Either regarded as sacred or demonized, it functions as an absolute. It positions us within the eternity of Nature, which imposes itself on us from the outside:

> The starting point of these reflections was usually a feeling of impatience at the sight of the "naturalness" with which newspapers, art and common sense constantly dress up a reality which, even though it is the one we live in, is undoubtedly determined by history. In short, in the account given of our contemporary circumstances, I resented seeing Nature and History confused at every turn, and I wanted to track down, in the decorative display of *what-goes-without-saying*, the ideological abuse which, in my view, is hidden there.[10]

This is what Roland Barthes writes at the beginning of *Mythologies*. In the postface he specifies: "In passing from history to nature, myth acts economically: it abolishes the complexity of human acts, it gives them the simplicity of essences, it does away with all dialectics, with any going back beyond what is immediately visible, it organizes a world which is without contradictions since it is without depth, a world wide open and wallowing in the evident, it establishes a blissful clarity; things appear to mean something by themselves."[11]

The beings caught up in this process of reification, arrested in this petrification, are reduced to "the arbitrariness of an ideogram." Thus, according to *Mythologies*, the image on the cover of *Paris-Match* in which we see a young black saluting the French flag does not refer us back to his biography as an African, nor to his individual truth. It effaces these in order to signify all at once, to force us to translate: "France is a great empire." It is both the imposition of an idea and the training of a reflex. Barthes' analyses mostly concern right-wing myths. They also encompass a few left-wing myths, like the mythification of Stalin:

> Stalin, as a spoken object, has exhibited for years, in their pure state, the constituent characters of mythical speech: a meaning, which was the real Stalin, that of history; a signifier, which was the ritual invocation to Stalin, and the *inevitable* character of the "natural" epithets with which his name was surrounded; a signified, which was the intention to respect orthodoxy, discipline and unity, *appropriated* by the Communist parties to a definite situation; and a signification, which was a sanctified Stalin, whose historical determinants found themselves grounded in nature, sublimated under the name of Genius, that is, something irrational and inexpressible: here, depoliticization is evident, it fully reveals the presence of a myth.[12]

The utterance — "Stalin is a genius" — is supposed to roll off the tongue as an immediate, unquestionable truth. Similarly, the consumer of pamphlets (or rumors, or satirical engravings) does not dissociate the character of the wife of Louis XVI from a fixed sign, an ideogram indicating that Marie-Antoinette is a monster.

What Barthes says about the discourse of his times is also valid for this wild and lewd fresco in which in pamphlet after pamphlet the person of the queen is painted as "the agent of all the vices." The feverish denunciation of one woman's bad character conceals complex political and historical stakes about which the French have every reason to be divided. The outrageous perversities of a foreign woman soiling the throne of France, already putrid from so many sins, provoked universal condemnation (and happened to help while away sleepless nights). To read these lampoons as if

they "go without saying" and refer directly to an existing reality —
the vicious temperament of the Austrian Woman (misogyny and
xenophobia being the two essential elements from which spring,
according to an identical thematic, the royalist as well as the revolutionary pamphlets attacking the queen) — seems to me proof
of a naïveté, either real or feigned, that deliberately confuses the
production of a language with natural fact, or else ignores the dimension of *myth* itself.

Now, the function of these proliferating lampoons was precisely to elaborate a mythology, and it did so with the cold profes-
sionalism and strategic precision of any commercial writing. The
Monster-Queen presented by them, the Unnameable endlessly
declaimed in untiring rites of execration, ruled over a divided world
of excess — a universe, lacking nuance, or any possible movement
between good and evil. Marie-Antoinette, the Foreign Woman,
Messalina, Proserpine, was evil, a fiend from hell. Confronting
her, opposing the evil queen who will stop at nothing, were the
combined forces of good, of the New World which can only be
born of itself.

The image of Marie-Antoinette as the Wicked Queen had the
power to unify. It gave substance to an enemy painted in the colors of the Devil. And the latter, as we know, is light-footed: "The
ground is strewn for the Sabbath, here one treads only on feathers."

It became all the more crucial to oppose her seductive ma-
noeuvers with eternal vigilance, and her obscenities with sick-
ened reprobation. With one voice, the chorus of the people cursed
the Queen. The myth was all the more powerful because it cast
the diabolical queen in the role of Eve, seduced and seductive, exploiting Adam's weakness to ensure that the Devil's plans succeed.

The royal pair are thus conflated with the Biblical couple: At
the side of a cruel and all-powerful queen, Louis XVI, the good but
weak king, was supported by public opinion until his flight to

Varennes in June 1791. (That too is the fault of the queen, aided by Fersen, but this time the king has gone too far in his submissiveness to his wife.) Guilt was laid squarely on the queen's head.

Louis XVI was good, too good. For a sovereign, the line between goodness and imbecility was easily crossed. With an imaginative and tirelessly orgiastic energy, and in all possible positions, the people-king fornicated with the queen, doing everything to her the king himself was too impotent to do.

That the myth of Marie-Antoinette's erotic superpowers — associated with a genius for evil defying human capability — met with the sanction of the real is astonishing. In the absence of any proof of her political treason, the queen was judged according to the pornographic fantasies of a whole nation. Take the example of the pamphlet, *Love Under Siege, or the Last Pleasures of Marie-Antoinette: A Comedy in 3 Acts, in prose, staged for the first time at the Temple, August 20, 1792*. The curtain rises with a tête-à-tête between Marie-Antoinette and Lafayette who, since the October Days of 1789, has become her preferred sexual partner, according to the pamphleteer. He has relieved the king's brother, the comte d'Artois, incomparable "athlete of pleasure" who had made Toinon [Antoinette] swoon so many times. A short visit from her son put the queen in a bad mood: "The little bastard said nothing foul!" She nicely regained her ardor thanks to the caresses of the princesse de Lamballe. Warmed up, she decides to go further and see — the very height of perversity — "what a commoner's balls can do." The princess encouraged the happy Dubois, who was foolishly intimidated: "Follow me. Stick it in her throat, even up her arse. You can do anything you like...."

In accordance with a system of references characteristic of the marginal literature of the pamphlets, a note at the end of the volume reads: "To prove the authenticity of the facts I have just revealed to the public, I invite the reader to glance through *The*

Libertine and Scandalous Private Life of Marie-Antoinette, 3-volumes-in-18, with 32 illustrations; a rare book, entirely true, whose principal anecdotes are known only to a few, notably the third volume recently published."[13]

What is astonishing is that no one is astonished that such tales, endlessly taken up and embellished with new depravities, could ever (and continue to) seem plausible; that, even though they are considered exaggerated, the assumption remains that real events can be traced or authentic persons investigated *on the basis of the pamphlets alone.* To absolve or condemn Marie-Antoinette on the basis of the scandal sheets directed against her amounts to accepting a natural transition between strategically manipulated fantasy which casts its heroine in the image of evil, and Marie-Antoinette's factual existence, which would correspond more or less to the myth created about her.

In the eighteenth century, the same abusive correlation between myth and reality, between imagined and lived scenes, made an author legally responsible for the immorality of his characters. Thus the Marquis de Sade, after spending thirteen years in prison, was incarcerated in the Hospice de Charenton, where he was condemned to remain from 1801 until his death in 1814, by the scandalous nature of his published work. He was locked away for producing on paper monsters of wickedness violently committed, like Marie-Antoinette of the pamphlets, to the triumph of crime.

If Sade's name is introduced here, it's because there are echoes and disturbing links between the sexual violence of the pamphlets and Sade's writing: in the pamphlets, the same ludicrous character was often expressed in fanciful inscriptions and editorial notes. In the play of inscriptions, the similarity between Sade and the revolutionary pamphlets is clear. The cruel and ironic sentence, "Mothers should make this prescribed reading for their daughters," which Sade placed at the head of *Philosophy in the Bedroom*

19

(1795), echoes an identical epigraph in a pamphlet that appeared in 1791, *The Uterine Furors of Marie-Antoinette, Wife of Louis XVI*; the pamphlet's imprint was: "At the Riding School,[14] and in all the brothels of Paris."

Finally, it seems to me that the destinies of Sade and Marie-Antoinette were in a certain way homologous. They were both, in all senses of the term, victims of dreams. The condemnation of each arose from the same lack of distinction between person and text. They were both overtaken by the phantasmic power they unleashed, the one as author, the other as personality. Sade paid the penalty for the heinous crimes of his characters Noirceuil, Saint-Fond, Juliette, and Clairwill, who are capable of offering such gems as "Ah! How sweet crime is and how voluptuous afterward!" Marie-Antoinette paid the penalty for the flagrant infamy of the bitch she incarnates in the pamphlets, the woman who proclaims, "In Olympus, in Hades, I want to fuck everywhere" — and does so.

The radical politician and revolutionary journalist Hébert's charge of incest against Marie-Antoinette — which left her speechless before she was obliged to reply, "I appeal to all mothers who may be present" — was directly inspired by the pages of the scandal sheets. For years, these texts had painted her as an adulteress, traitor, sodomite, lesbian, incestuous mother, infant murderess, and so on. Marie-Antoinette, in any case, didn't like to read; she could not have cared less about such depictions and she never could see the relationship between herself and the Infernal Shrew. Yet that relationship was never in doubt for the reader of the pamphlets. So it was with confidence that the president of the tribunal, speaking after the witnesses' (by definition) concrete and verifiable testimony, denounced "the infernal machinations of this modern Medici." Marie-Antoinette, the widow Capet, summoned (out of declared respect for the principle of equality) before the revolutionary tribunal, continued to be identified with the extraordinary mythic figure she had become. Myth has a life of its own, based on an internal logic, a conventional, profoundly oneiric imagery. It is independent of its support: the latter may die the physical death of the body, but the myth still hovers over the cadaver.

It is this type of mythic speech as it was applied to Marie-Antoinette with remarkable eloquence, insistence, and passion, that I propose to present and analyze here, and I will do so without taking sides. I am not taking up proceedings but describing a trajectory, following a life, not in its effective biography but in that powerfully resonating space, with its blurred contours but all too concrete effects, where gossip, rumor, and calumny take shape. For me it is not a question of resurrecting a character, for Marie-Antoinette has never ceased to inspire biographies, from the Goncourt brothers' to Stefan Zweig's, right up to the recent books by Evelyne Lever and Jean Chalon. The stories of her life, mostly written with sympathy, if not with love, are numerous. By looking at the unreal double that Marie-Antoinette very quickly became for the French public opinion of her time, I am trying to define what killed her, to trace the ever darker contours of her image (as a horror film might show the transformation of a young princess into a prostitute, a nymphomaniac, a vampire, a monster).

Whatever else, her story is a *roman noir*. And for Marie-Antoinette's judges to have made no distinction between the charges of the scandal sheets with which they had been intoxicated for years and those they laid against her at the time of her trial made her death sentence the true monstrosity.

Revolution and Misogyny

The violence of the scandal sheets, which prolonged itself and fulfilled itself in Marie-Antoinette's death sentence, was violence

21

against the reign of pleasure as privilege, and of pleasure as feminine. Marie-Antoinette at Versailles, and even more so at the Trianon, was the first queen of France to break with the tradition of self-effacement to which the wives of Louis XIV or Louis XV had submitted before her. She was the first to lend Versailles her style, to impose her imprint on it, and to promulgate the dictates of fashion. Under Louis XIV or Louis XV, this initiatory role belonged to the king or his favorite. Such visibility places Marie-Antoinette in line with the great courtesans. It was first under this title (leaving aside the detested title of "Austrian" to a people for whom Austria had been a hereditary enemy) that she drew the arrows of the lampoonists. Handled with a perfidiousness not without irony during the ancien régime, the arrows grew in number and in brutality during the revolutionary years. The Revolution, as the work of Lynn Hunt has established,[15] had a "homosocial," masculine ideal of virtue.[16] Its iconographic repertoire clearly spoke of this choice, which was doubled, in principle as in practice, by a systematic exclusion of women. There were flaws, certainly, but these arose from a conception of woman so traditional and so reductive that they only intensified the seclusion of women, not their liberation.

The first such flaw was the acceptance of women into groups as demonstrators. (Women triumph, according to this view, on the day of October 6, 1789, in the course of which they "bring back" the royal family to Paris.)[17] Here we need only look at the way the radical journalist Jean-Paul Marat, nicknamed "the Friend of women," glorified them — never as individuals but as an indistinct mass made strong by the emotional and vital energy animating them, by their essential spontaneity. The second flaw in this system of exclusion, one omnipresent in revolutionary rhetoric and in the festivals consecrating it, was the praise of women as *wives and mothers*, that is, as women dedicated and devoted to the

Citizens whose companions they were, and to those Citizens to come whose mothers they would be. Such wives and mothers were revolutionary in their capacity for suffering in their generous self-effacement as mere links in the generational chain, bridges thrown across to the regenerated people. The Romantic historian Michelet, a fanatic champion of the weak and suffering woman who is unable to survive outside the contract of helpmate that binds her to her man, wrote: "Women were at the forefront of our Revolution. There is nothing surprising about that. They suffered more."[18] He described their thirst for heroics in these terms: "They look around them to see where the heroes of Plutarch might be; they want them, they will create them."[19] In a perfectly analogous spirit, linking femininity, maternity and the sacrificial vocation, Mona Ozouf declares: "The child [...] was of major political importance: by him alone could the Revolution triumph. And thus, by women alone."[20] Ozouf defends "the lovely title" of such "citizen spouses": "It is true," she notes, "that women could no longer hold the cards. But their role was to watch the game over the player's shoulder, to advise him discreetly, to share his success, to console his misfortunes."[21]

One easily recognizes here Jean-Jacques Rousseau's vision of women. Rousseau consigned women to the enclosed space of the hearth and feared like the plague their presence in the public sphere, in particular the sphere of intellectual exchange (nothing equals Rousseau's horror of women writers) and circulating desire. Thus in *Emile or On Education* (1762), considering the case of Sophie — the young girl he wants his pupil to marry — Rousseau raised mediocrity to the level of a virtue:

> Therefore, it is not suitable for a man with education to take a wife who has none, or, consequently, to take a wife from a rank in which she could not have an education. But I would still like a simple and

23

coarsely raised girl a hundred times better than a learned and brilliant one who would come to establish in my house a tribunal of literature over which she would preside. A brilliant wife is a plague to her husband, her children, her friends, her valets, everyone.[...] Desire mediocrity in everything, without excepting even beauty. An attractive and prepossessing for that inspires not love but benevolence is what one ought to prefer.[22]

This bourgeois conception is haunted by the specter of the plot, by the imaginary threat of the sect. "Women among themselves" are, for Rousseau as for Diderot, abomination itself. Their mutual proximity compounds the enigma harbored within each. As a group they escape all control (meaning masculine control), indulge in forbidden games, give free rein to their innate sense of treachery. Diderot, in his brief and dazzling essay, "On Women," wrote: "Impenetrable in dissimulation, cruel in vengeance, persevering in their schemes, unscrupulous in the methods they employ, animated by a profound and secret hatred of male despotism, they seem linked by a loose plot for domination, in a sort of league such as that which subsists between the priests of every country; they know the articles of their bond without its having to be first communicated to them."[23]

The literature of the pamphlets feeds on this fantasy of a *league*, headed by a woman symbolizing absolute power and pleasure, dominating the public sphere and reserving for herself all the rights of the private. The Women of the House of the Queen ("the Tribades of Versailles," as the lampoonists call them) played a central role here. What was targeted through Marie-Antoinette was the specter of a triumphant feminine liberty, playful and pleasurable, the image of a sovereignty existing only through and for itself, not needing to justify itself through some relationship to Man or Child. The latter were in any case only justified in revolutionary ideology through their relationship to the Nation. Such an ideology was obviously more fluid and progressive, especially in relation to women. Mona Ozouf rightly underlines the positive value and even boldness of certain propositions of the Revolution on the civil status of woman. We might recall Condorcet's *Essai sur l'admission des femmes au droit de cité* (1790) or the Law of September 20, 1792 on divorce, according to which, "One of the spouses can have divorce pronounced based on the simple allegation of incompatibility of humour or of character." Revolutionary indeed, this law was based on a new conception of marriage. As Francis Ronsin sees it: "Outside its religious signification, the marriage of the Ancien Régime was generally conceived as a treaty of alliance between two families. With divorce, the Revolution invents the couple: an association with an egalitarian vocation, based on reciprocal affection, concluded and, if possible, perpetuated in freedom."[24] I realize the problem I touch on here is complex. I pose it only in so far as the "case of Marie-Antoinette" is revealing from a symbolic and fantasmatic point of view. And from this point of view, the scandal sheets against the queen are damning. Marie-Antoinette was fantasized as the incarnation of an extreme debauchery. A collective delirium developed over the effigy she had become, eschewing any attention to the person herself.

Mme de Staël, daughter of ex-comptroller General Jacques Necker and soon to be one of France's great Romantic novelists, reacted against such misogynist rage when, in August 1793, she published her *Réflexions sur le procès de la Reine*. In its style and rhetoric, as a gestural and emotional outburst, this impassioned text closely resembles a speech for the defense. It testified to a realization that forced Mme de Staël, in the name of sheer justice, to move beyond her own political and personal sympathies. She vigorously asserted that "no queen, during the period of her omnipotence has ever seen herself libelled so publicly." She insisted on the suffering Marie-Antoinette endured as a mother: "I come back to you, all you women sacrificed in a mother so tender, all of you sacrificed by the attack that would be committed against frailty, by the annihilation of pity; your empire is done for if ferocity reigns, your fate is doomed if your tears fall in vain. Defend the queen with all the arms of nature; go and find the child that will perish if he loses the one who has loved him so."[25]

Réflexions sur le procès de la Reine was signed simply "By a Woman." The anonymity fooled no one. Readers recognized Necker's daughter who was herself the target of lampoonists. Useless as a cautionary measure, this anonymity designated as closely as possible the affiliation revindicated by the author. It spoke intimately of the indignation behind it. The same call to a community of women, all humiliated in the person of Marie-Antoinette, led the feminist and revolutionary Olympe de Gouges, to publish her *Déclaration des droits de la Femme et de la Citoyenne, dédiée à la Reine* in 1791.

The hooker of Austria

CHAPTER ONE

The Hostage Princesses

"Being a queen is not the happiest condition in the world. I wouldn't have wanted to be one for anything. You suffer the worst restrictions, you have no power whatsoever, you are like an idol: you must put up with everything and somehow be happy regardless."[1] Elisabeth Charlotte, Liselotte to her nearest and dearest, daughter of the prince elector of the Palatinate, wife of Monsieur, Louis XIV's brother, wrote these disabused sentences on the queenly state in a letter dated March 16, 1719. One can take her at her word without reading her declaration as a sign of secret frustration or unsatisfied vanity. In 1719, Elisabeth Charlotte was sixty-seven years old. She had lived at Versailles since she was nineteen and knew the miseries that were the obverse of power, the welter of constraints and humiliations that go hand in hand with the splendor of even the grandest moments — especially for women. The letters of the princesse Palatine constitute a precious testimony, because she was an amazing writer and was a rebel to the end (despite Louis XIV, who, with absolute despotism, ruled over even the slightest actions and decisions of his family).

Nothing could stop the princesse Palatine's insolence, or, in the words of the king, shut her "great gob." Nothing ever diminished her energy or her forthright behavior. When her son,

Philippe d'Orléans, the future regent, told her of his marriage to one of Louis XIV's bastards, she slapped his face, in public. She burst out laughing on seeing a lady who had come to visit her trip over one of her dogs and nearly fall into the fire. And again, when Louis XIV, after one of the numerous deaths that succeeded each other at Versailles toward the end of his reign, forbade signs of mourning, she yielded to grief and bawled her eyes out — but without dropping out of the stag hunt. Such a strong personality made the limitations of the feminine role (essentially reproductive and decorative) to which she was destined intolerable: "I've regretted being a woman all my life, and, to tell the truth, I would have been better off as an elector[2] than a Madame."[3]

Married to the king's brother, known as Monsieur, a declared homosexual, she accomplished her task as breeder in order to perpetuate a name, but no more. She gave birth to three children, two of whom did not count: the first died at an early age and the other was a girl. The third, happily for Monsieur, who could now resume his sexual habits, was a son. The couple stopped sleeping in the same room, and Madame's sex life ended. "If it is possible to recover your virginity after not sleeping with your husband for nineteen years, then I have definitely become a virgin again," she wrote ironically, if not bitterly, years later.[4]

It is exclusively as breeders, their sole function in continuing a dynasty, that women appear in the gazettes of the time. They are only of interest for the nine months of their pregnancies. They are then mentioned in between accounts of the glorious exploits of men in battle, or after accounts of the travels in which men educate and entertain themselves. In *La Gazette d'Amsterdam*, *La Gazette de Leyde*, for example, or in *Le Courrier de L'Europe*, one may read news items of this ilk: "Yesterday morning, all the ladies of the court had the honor of kissing the hand of Mme la Grande Duchesse, who has returned from her confinement, and of complimenting Her Royal Highness on the occasion, as is the custom." Or: "Recently, Mme the comtesse d'Artois had the misfortune to fall on her knees. Although the fall was not a bad one, it nonetheless caused the court great concern for the princess's pregnancy." Or else: "The King of Spain has arrived at the palace of Aranjuez with the royal family; Mme the Princess of Asturias appeared a little tired from the journey. His Majesty has decreed that, in all the churches, in Aranjuez as in Madrid, public prayers will be said for the safe delivery of Her Royal Highness, who is coming to the end of the term of her pregnancy." And so on. When women are not pregnant, there is little to say about them.

As for the decorative role, the princesse Palatine was unfit. She was ugly, ill disposed to coquetry, and intolerant of the waste of time and energy that a woman was expected to devote to her clothing. Her natural ugliness was further aggravated by pock marks, which is why she eventually refused to sit for portraits. This ugliness, which she discussed with perfect detachment, removed her from the sphere of feverish rituals dominating court life. All the celebrations, balls, marriages, and so on were for her so many chores that she must grin and bear. She was never dispossessed by the gaze of onlookers, never experienced the giddiness of being admired. And so she remained in control of looking.

Her letters depict the court as a prison, an airless, dangerous place governed equally by the play of pride and mad lying, where the most serious financial dependency and a permanent state of debt lay hidden behind dazzling expenditure. On the first of January each year after the death of her husband, she received her yearly stipend from the king. A few days later, after paying her debts, she was once again completely broke. Beneath the official image of princesses and queens, seldom questioned and more often envied, she revealed an existence of isolation, stifled tears, and repression. Reading her, it becomes easier to understand the strange contrast, in the portraits of queens, between the glorious gowns and finery and the dead faces, which neither look nor smile — faces that are simply submissive.

Reasons of state, as we know, determined a prince's choice of spouse. The constraint, for him, hardly mattered. He had no need to confuse love and political alliance. It would have been perfectly ridiculous to do so. The story was different for a young woman. Not that she had to love her husband — her duty did not extend that far. But she was entirely dependent on him and not free to love elsewhere. While still an adolescent, the fiancée was torn from her family, her country, her mother tongue. She found herself on enemy ground, delivered as the hostage in a pact concluded between her father and the father of her future lord and master. This traffic in foreign girls, who arrived decked out like icons and to whom all possible homages were paid, was conducted with indifference and cynicism, motivated by purely political calculation. These girls were the guarantee of alliances whose stakes they did not understand. All they knew when they left their childhood homes was that they would never return.

Just about all of them were desperate, but rare were those who described this with the vigor of the princesse Palatine, who wrote to her aunt, the duchess of Hanover, "When Mme de Wartenberg told Dondorff that I screamed so much I nearly busted a gut, she was telling the truth, for all I did was scream all night from Strasbourg to Châlons. I couldn't bear the thought of leaving those who had come to say good-bye...."[5]

To cite another example of a woman determined not to give in, or at least to express her opposition, we might mention the amazing Frederick Sophie Wilhelmina (1709–58), daughter of the king of Prussia, sister of Frederick the Great. For a time, there was talk of her marrying the future king of England. One day an envoy from her potential fiancé arrived in Berlin, from London. The little girl was "drawn out of her hole" and examined by candlelight. She did not say a word to the envoy. Her mother, the queen, made a terrible fuss. Frederick Sophie Wilhelmina writes in her *Mémoires*: "I withdrew in tears to my room; I was outraged with the queen and with [the fiancé]. I swear I will never wed the king of England; if they were willing to put me so thoroughly under his thumb before the marriage, I was well aware that I would be worse than a slave once it was under contract."[6] She later adds: "I maintained that a good union should be founded on reciprocal esteem and consideration."[7] Mistreated by her parents, starving, beaten, the young girl succeeded in making the marriage of her choice, but only by pure accident. Her resistance had nothing to do with it. Her husband of choice was approved only after negotiations with England had failed.

More often, young princesses would just grin and bear it, joining in the welcoming festivities as much as they could manage, regardless of their anguish. A good example is Louis XV's wife, Marie Leszczynska, daughter of the Polish king, whom the courtiers, deploring the misalliance with a woman whose name was unpronounceable, called "the Polack." After her father, who had accompanied her on horseback, left her without a word to avoid the agony of parting, she resigned herself to continuing to France alone. She leaned out the door of the carriage and found no one there.

In terms of theatrical border crossings, however, nothing compares with the ceremonial "handing over" of Marie-Antoinette to France. A building was specially designed for this ritual which evokes the idea of an initiation as well as the frisking of a convict. Built on an island in the Rhine between Kehl and Strasbourg, it contained four rooms. Two faced the left bank: Marie-Antoinette entered these, with her train, as the archduchess of Austria. Two faced the right bank: here the archduchess was transformed into the dauphine of France. In order for this metamorphosis to be achieved, she had to cross an invisible but irrevocable line, after being stripped of everything — clothes, jewelry, shoes, ribbons. The dauphine could not retain any trace of her past life, nor could any of the women in her entourage. She arrived, alone and naked, on what symbolically represented French soil. At the end of the ceremony she broke down and cried in the arms of her new lady-in-waiting, Mme de Noailles. ("Ask M. and Mme de Noailles," her mother advised her, "in fact, demand, in all circumstances, what you should do as a foreigner who absolutely desires to please the nation."[8]) For the first few months, that is what Marie-Antoinette did; but very quickly exasperated, she then dreamed only of escaping the woman she nicknamed "Mme Etiquette." Of Mme de Noailles, Mme Campan writes, not without nostalgia for a lost world, "etiquette was to her a sort of atmosphere; at the slightest derangement of the consecrated order, one would have thought she would have been stifled."[9]

It was not easy adjusting to such a milieu. The princesse Palatine found it suffocating: "I must say they are absolutely full of themselves here," she proclaimed on entering the rarefied atmosphere of the court. Marie-Antoinette, by contrast, sought to escape it by carving out some private niche for herself. Others, like the conscientious Marie Leszczynska, spent their whole lives struggling not to make mistakes, to make people forget that they were foreigners.

Is it possible to imagine anyone more defenseless than these young exiles, confronted by a court protocol which in itself comprised a whole new language to learn on top of French? Their faux pas were mocked, their mistakes in French and their confusion over titles mimicked. Marie Thérèse, Louis XIV's wife, never shed her thick Spanish accent. "Our good late queen spoke a most peculiar French. For a start, there was never a 'u'; everything was 'ou.' Moreover, she used to say *servillieta* for *serviette* [towel], *Sancta Biergen* for *Sainte Vierge* [Holy Virgin], *escevois* for *cheveux* [hair], and a dozen other similar mistakes."[10] The princesse Palatine, noting the hispanisms of Marie Thérèse, cultivated her Germanisms and did all she could to preserve them. She never lost her accent either, which made her say, and even write, for instance, *Pastille* for *Bastille*. (Marie-Antoinette, on the other hand, rapidly lost practically all traces of her accent. She got *la Bastille* right; even at the height of emotion, she never said "the taking of the Pastille"!)

During her sad existence, Marie Thérèse had plenty to complain about to the "Sancta Biergen." Biographers still use a contemptuous tone in perpetuating her memory. She is described as "good and pious, but wonderfully credulous and silly; she does nothing but play cards, nibble, and get fat all day. In memory of Spain, she stuffs herself with garlic and swallows cup after cup of chocolate, which, in the opinion of the ladies of the court, makes her teeth go black." This melancholia-induced bulimia was no cause for mockery. It should be viewed in the light of her last words, uttered on her deathbed: "All my life, for as long as I've been queen, I haven't really had one single day of happiness...."

Day after day, Louis XIV's wife missed Spain, her homeland; but for a French princess, the court of Spain was hell. The princesse Palatine wrote about the early days of Marie Louise d'Orléans (the daughter of her husband and Henrietta of England, his first wife) as queen of Spain: "I received letters from her only today; from what I understand from these letters and the stories people here have brought back with them, Spain must be the most frightful place on earth; the manners there are incredibly insipid and tedious. Poor child! I feel for her with all my heart, obliged to spend the rest of her life in such a country. The only consolation will be the little dogs she took with her. The court has already started her on a regimen of *seriousness* so severe that she is no longer allowed to speak to her former equerry; she may only wave and nod at him, and that only in passing."[11]

In addition to the systematic program of "seriousness" and isolation, there was also the program of humiliation, very much in vogue at Versailles since it provided entertainment for the courtiers. When taken to extremes, and with enough inventiveness, it was literally murderous. That is what happened to Marie Anne of Bavaria-Neuburg, Louis XIV's daughter-in-law: "The poor dauphine is sick again. She is now in the hands of a monk they call Brother Angel. They are killing her with heartache. They do all they can to reduce her to such a state; but I am a harder nut to crack than Mme la Dauphine."[12]

Even those who pleased the court, in the beginning, because of their charm or the element of novelty they introduced into the routine of court life, quickly became boring. If they were not set upon to be "broken" they were forgotten, left to their perpetual labors as breeders, the only task required of them. Catherine de' Medici, after failing to bear children for ten years because of an anatomical defect in Henry, produced eleven pregnancies and ten children, leaving the king plenty of spare time for Diane de Poitiers. At the beginning of her reign, Marie Leszczynska had nine children in nine years. A pretty stupid career, as the princesse Palatine said, and all the more so since, though neglected as people (existing only insofar as they were fecund), they no less represented a foreign power, and a virtually hostile one at that. They were watched like spies.[13] Their correspondence was censored. Such police tactics enraged the princesse Palatine, who, not much given to moderating her language (she detested Mme de Maintenon, whom she calls "the pantécrate," "that old bag," "the old sea-hag," "Mme Shitface," and so on), addressed her censor directly:

"This morning I had the great pleasure of receiving two packets from my aunt at once. What astounded me was that the first had been opened in Hanover itself; to top it off, they made me a real doozy of a letter, since, to prove that both letters had been read, they mixed the pages up. Only a drunk could have done such a job, so I imagine it was Count Platen; he has only to read the letter I'm writing today to get his deserts...."[14]

Less provocative, shrewder, and more inclined, given her seductive temperament, to model her replies on the expectations and desires of her interlocutor, Marie-Antoinette nonetheless complained of never being safe from informers: "Mme la Dauphine does not feel any note is safe at home. She worries about duplicate keys; she is frightened that they come and take hers in the middle of the night."[15]

Hostage princesses slept with one eye open. At court, that bastion of honors and flattery, scene of the latest dances, a state of war was forever brewing, and they risked being its first victims at any given moment. When the princesse Palatine arrived at Versailles, she knew that she was succeeding Henrietta of England, who, according to sound sources, had been poisoned by one of her husband's male lovers. As soon as the empress of Austria learned that her daughter was pregnant, she warned Marie-Antoinette to beware of poison.

This incessant harrassment combining politics and emotions with official representations was exhausting. It was a war of attrition from which a woman rarely emerged victorious. (At one time, the princesse Palatine could not even talk to her children in privacy: "If I say two words to my children, they have to endure half an hour's interrogation so that what I said may be discovered."[16]) Not to lose oneself completely was indeed an achievement. As for freedom, it was useless even to think about it. After long years of dedicated resistance, even the princesse Palatine admitted defeat: "They have clipped my wings so badly — and deliberately at that — that even if I were master of my own fate, I would not get very far."[17] This capitulation was indeed more moving and more terrible than a general's unconditional surrender, for the princess lost an absolutely solitary struggle, ending a state of war all the more fearsome for never having been declared.

I opened this text, which in its own way tells of the execution of a queen, with a homage to the princesse Palatine because she alone in the history of queens and princesses speaks, even shouts, about the true status of these women, obliging us to recognize the vigilance and intelligence they needed to withstand the pressures to which they were subjected or the indifference in which they vegetated. When one thinks of Marie-Antoinette, "the Austrian Woman," whom the Revolution held hostage, and then eliminated, one should bear in mind just how difficult her position was. Such is what determines at the outset the behavior and feelings of a queen, however romantic she may be. Marie-Antoinette had no choice in her relations with Louis XVI. She had to make an ally of him, and she did everything in her power to succeed. ("The most satisfying thing for Mme la Dauphine," wrote the Austrian ambassador to France and confidante of the queen, Mercy-Argenteau, "is that she gains ascendancy daily over the mind of the dauphin. With a bit of care she will no doubt manage to subjugate him completely."[18]) Did she love the king or didn't she? The question is almost meaningless, as Marie-Antoinette was well aware, declaring to her mother, not without fatalism, "I am sure that if I had to choose between the three of them [the three brothers, Louis XVI, the Comte de Provence, and the Comte d'Artois], I would still choose the one God gave me...."[19]

By the same token, Marie-Antoinette's friendship with the handsome Swedish courtier Count of Fersen, which makes sensitive souls reel, should also be seen in terms of a political strategy. After the king's death, Fersen's support was indissociable from the project of restoring royalty, which would have made Marie-Antoinette the regent and reserved a decisive role for Fersen. Far from being a romantic hero or a character in a pastoral, the Swedish aristocrat was first and foremost a cold, stubborn power-broker. Only his exceptional good looks would allow him to be passed off as a character in a novel. In contrast, the tone of his diary reveals no flurry of emotion. It is even, precise, mournful. Fersen has only one obsession: "good company." His timetable gives the impression of a whirlwind of frivolity, acted out against a backdrop of boredom and melancholia. Here, for example, is what he wrote in his journal during his first trip to Paris:

> The 1st of January, 1774, being New Year's Day, I had to go to Versailles to pay my respects to the king and watch the ceremony of the Order of the Holy Spirit. I sent for my carriage at eight o'clock, but I was obliged to wait, cursing like a fool, until eight forty-five, for the tailor to bring me a fur coat that I had had him make the day before yesterday; I was at Versailles by ten o'clock. The ceremony is just a mass in which the king and all the knights participate dressed in ceremonial garb. After dining, I went with Count Creuts to pay Mme du Barry a visit; she spoke to me then for the first time. When we left, we returned to Paris, and I went home and lay down, rather tired.

Fersen never married. He turned down several offers, one of whom was the future Mme de Staël. Fersen evokes his possible fiancée in these terms: "I only saw her once in passing and I don't remember her face. I recall only that she was not at all disagreeable and that she was not deformed...."

In Sweden he was the acknowledged chief of the upper aristocracy and a fierce opponent of any form of democracy. The French Revolution and the death of the queen only served to reinforce the rigidity of his convictions. That is why, in the eyes of the people, he represented the enemy to be slain after the Swedish Revolution of 1809 and the deposition of King Gustav IV. For the Swedish people, he was the very incarnation of arrogance and aristocratic splendor, precisely as Marie-Antoinette had been for the French. On June 20, 1810, during the funeral for the prince of Augustenbourg, whom rumor has it Fersen killed, the crowd beat him to death. In a fit of collective fury, he was stoned, struck with canes and umbrellas, covered in mud and spit, stomped on, and ripped apart. On his person a menacing letter was found: "Although that arrogant aristocrat, your miserable father, managed to get away with his crimes, although he used the vilest means to get rich at the expense of his country, although your long neck, supporting that brainless little head, was able to escape the French guillotine, although your sister, the poisoner, has been spared the ax of justice until now, although your boundless pride has not yet been destroyed, understand that what has not yet been done can still be done. A country in the jaws of the fury of despair is a terrible thing."

Did Marie-Antoinette love Fersen or didn't she? I don't have the answer. I can only underscore how very close their public images and their political destinies were.

Queens in history books are not to be confused with fairytale queens. The diamonds sparkling on their crowns blind us to the reality of the political stresses their marriages' sanction — and for which certain cautious liaisons, rarely, offer consolation.

It is this reality that triumphs with open brutality when, after divorcing Joséphine de Beauharnais, Napoleon envisaged a second marriage, no longer of love but of convenience. Anticipating rejection by the czar, he renounced his interest in the czar's daughter, the Grand Duchess Anne, and looked to Austria, his enemy of the last eleven years. "Tomorrow night," he commanded his minister of foreign affairs, "you will send a second letter [to Petersburg] to let them know I've decided on *the Austrian woman* [emphasis added]." This is Marie Louise, archduchess of Austria, granddaughter of Marie Caroline of Naples and, thus, great-grand-niece of Marie-Antoinette, who is so elegantly referred to.

So that contempt for the founding sacrifices of the Revolution and the farce of legitimacy could be taken to the limit, the marriage contract sent to Vienna was an exact copy of Louis XVI and Marie-Antoinette's. And to celebrate the event, Gluck's *Iphigénie en Aulide* was performed at the Opera, in front of the emperor of Germany, Franz II, and his entire court. Its first performance in Paris in 1774 had been a personal triumph for Marie-Antoinette. Seated next to her father, the future bride had listened to Agamemnon singing, on stage, of the pain of having to sacrifice his daughter:

You decide your fate:
Your brazen daring
Hastens the blow that menaces her;
She will be put to death.
Have at me, soldiers . . . Oh God! What am I to do?
It's your own daughter, cruel man, you're handing over;
Your daughter, so dear to your heart, so long;
My heart is breaking:
No, let her live . . . Ah! What is this weakness?
To save her life, which the gods have ruled out,
Must I sacrifice the interests of Greece?

Marie Louise bade farewell to her father in Vienna. She was then greeted at the border by Caroline Murat, queen of Naples, who forced her to separate from her faithful friend and companion, Mme Lazansky. The archduchess of Austria was enthusiastically received in France, with big, joyful demonstrations in Strasbourg, Lunéville, and Nancy.

Napoleon awaited her in Compiègne, at the very spot where Louis XV and the dauphin came to greet Marie-Antoinette.

Lampoons and engravings develop the fantasy of free access to the queen's genitalia.

CHAPTER TWO

The Incorrigible

The Queen is Reprimanded in Vain

The written or spoken word of the pamphlets (the pamphlet is halfway between the oral and the written) had its own characteristics, of which emphasis is paramount. The pamphlet worked in hyperbole, using all the techniques of rhetorical excess, rejecting the half measure, neutrality. From the perspective of the gutter press, objectivity was only a hypocritical mode of partiality, a ruse of passion. The excessive style of the pamphleteer knew no limits. It had to always go a further step in evil. Always worse: this is the ascending curve that lampoon heroes' adventures must follow, a requirement sometimes producing felicitous effects that might inspire a cartoonist today. A pamphlet directed against abbé Maury who, after a career as a court abbot, became notorious during the Revolution for his eloquent and brazen defense of the monarchy — *The New Don Bugger in the National Assembly, or abbé Maury at the Brothel* — informs us how this "master of the art of fucking," having refined his teaching "for the queen, a thousand heroines, and several illustrious persons," has run out of pupils. He is saved by the National Assembly, where he finds new resources for his lubricious genius. But the "new national brothel of men and women" is far from satisfying abbé Maury's appetites, which is why, according to the libelist, "After fucking them all / He climbed onto the roof to bugger the cat...."

When, at his transgressive wit's end, the hack writer stumbled, he could always resort to repetition, trotting out the same old infamies. In the pamphlet as in the family (and the pamphlets insolently assert a feigned and disturbing familiarity), nothing is said only once. The same accusations were repeated ad infinitum, without any sense of boredom; on the contrary, they were dished out with an infantile sexual excitement that only intensifies. One never tired of reiterating endlessly the vices of the queen, of proclaiming them, singing them, describing them in detail to one's heart's content. Calumny, beginning as the circulation of gossip within the court, quickly spread throughout Paris. With the growing pamphlet trade centered on the Palais-Royal — property of the king's cousin, Philippe d'Orléans, who is known to have employed pamphleteers ("gutter writers," in Robert Darnton's phrase) to attack the royal family through calumny, thus tarnishing the radiance of its renown. Through the proliferation of newspapers, calumny became a burgeoning monster, destructive, devouring, threatening even those who imagined they controlled it and profited by it. Any excuse would do. The prince de Ligne, a faithful friend of the queen's, waxed indignant about the systematic bad faith of the process: "[if Marie-Antoinette] responds to the friendship of a few people who are most devoted to her, they say she's *in love*.... Her evening walks on the terrace, her rides on horseback in the Bois de Boulogne, even music in the Orangerie, appear *suspect*. Her most innocent pleasures appear *criminal*. She is nice to everyone and so is declared a coquette...."[1]

If calumny, the monster with a thousand eyes and a thousand voices, seized on the smallest details of the queen's existence in order to make them seem wicked, things did not seriously heat up — for real political stakes until Marie-Antoinette became pregnant for the first time, in 1777. War was declared from that moment on. The revolutionaries had only to take up where the royalists left off. Everything came together in the mythical and devastating character of the infernal queen. Calumny triumphed and reached its gleeful peak in 1785. That same year, Marie-Antoinette conducted her own personal battle to obtain the king's permission to put on and star in Beaumarchais's play *The Barber of Seville* in her private theater at Trianon. She played the part of Rosine. That same year, the Diamond Necklace Affair broke into public view.

The Diamond Necklace Affair was a huge swindle involving a diamond necklace valued at £1.8 million purchased in the queen's name. The crown jeweler, Boehmer, had tried unsuccessfully to sell the fabulous jewels to Louis XV for Mme du Barry. Now, the cardinal de Rohan, wanting to ingratiate himself to Marie-Antoinette, who had for a long time been hostile to him, took the dealings upon himself. He acquired the necklace from Boehmer and passed it on to his mistress, the comtesse Jeanne de La Motte, who immediately handed it over to her husband, who then ran off with it to try and sell the diamonds in England. This incredible scenario was principally the work of the comtesse de La Motte, this bold adventuress who had passed herself off to the cardinal de Rohan as a close personal friend of the queen's, with the power to reconcile him to her. Thus she persuaded him to serve as her intermediary in the purchase of the diamonds. When the fraud was discovered, the cardinal de Rohan was sent to the Bastille, along with the comte Cagliostro, the cardinal's familiar, and the comtesse de La Motte, who tried to shift the entire blame onto the cardinal. But to the amazement and horror of Marie-Antoinette, whose antipathy for the prelate blinded her to the story's complexity (even today many points remain obscure) and to the role played by the La Mottes, the Paris *parlement*'s verdict cleared the cardinal of forgery and fraud. He was, however, found guilty of lèse-majesté, for which he was banished from the royal court and stripped of his duties as grand chaplain. Although lenient, the verdict was wildly popular. All scorn and hatred seemed to fall on the queen. The comtesse de La Motte's sentence to be branded with an iron and sent to prison only added fuel to the fire of public animosity toward the queen. As Simon Schama writes:

> The real casualty of the whole affair was its principal victim: Marie-Antoinette (though the King's meanness in going through with the case was invidiously contrasted with the hapless Cardinal's sense of misplaced honor). Mysteriously, it was the Queen who emerged from the business portrayed as a spendthrift and a vindictive slut who would stop at nothing to satisfy her appetites. She had deliberately set out to destroy Rohan, it was said, because he would not respond to her indecent advances (an amazing scenario) and had spitefully manipulated de La Motte.... None of this would have been possible had there not already been a rich and unsavory vein of court pornography to tap.[2]

With the advent of freedom of the press in 1789, nothing could stop the sheer excess of the pamphleteers' fantasies of dirty deeds, their refinement of lurid detail, their enthusiasm for exposing the prostituted body of the queen. The pornographic imagination found in the saga of the queen's wickedness, pursued from one pamphlet to the next, a privileged form of expression. One of the most widely read pamphlets, which ran through several editions, *Historical Essays on the Life of Marie-Antoinette of Austria, Queen of France, to Serve as a History of this Princess* (1789), announced in the preface: "The incredible things you are about to read were not invented for pleasure; even if they are a little bit exaggerated for fun, at least the foundation is true."[3] Although the author finds pleasure in exaggerating, there is still a streak of truth — Marie-Antoinette's bad streak — which can always be drawn on to fuel new stories. And the reader is encouraged to do this, to develop at will the thumbnail sketches offered by the pamphlet: "It's not hard — anyone can add what he knows to what he is about to read — and who hasn't heard something?"[4]

Anything goes was the rule of the game. The pamphleteers made sport of finding the most poisonous barb, the most telling bit of muck, and the public imagination leapt to the task, experienced as it was in the political arena. The queen and her entourage were clearly the preferred targets of the revolutionary press, but the leaders of the Revolution used the same weapons against one another in their internal struggles, to such an extent that certain of them became alarmed and took the debate to the National Assembly. The victims of the scandal sheets complained that the boundary established between exaggeration and pure invention was insufficiently protected. For them the gutter press was all invention, and at a time when public opinion ruled supreme, the danger of such unbridled slander was patently clear. In January 1791, Malouet, addressing the assembly, demanded that all scandal sheets be prosecuted: "I say that with only partial measures, you will never eliminate the evil resulting from the unbridled licence ... of the press. I conclude that a law should be passed against the authors, printers, and hawkers of all lampoons, whatever they are, whose goal may be to bring the people to insurrection against the law."

Barnave opposed Malouet in these terms:

I would like to think and I am personally persuaded that those who are more attached to public concerns than to themselves would prefer the freedom of the press, even when it focuses on them, over any inconveniences that might ensue for their persons. Thus some through interest and others through love of freedom must feel that anything should be allowed to be said or printed about public figures, because the man who takes on public office necessarily exposes himself to censure, and no personal inconvenience can compare with the restraint that the law could impose on the expression of thought, which is the most sacred of all properties. Furthermore, public figures should not worry about the calumny that might be spread about them; this is always swept aside by their conduct and the freedom of action and opinion they safeguard.[5]

At the very moment that Barnave was defending the freedom of the press, the lampoonists had no qualms about printing whatever they liked (or disliked) about him. A stage direction in *The Patriotic Brothel* (1791), for example, tells us at the beginning of act 2 that "Barnave fucks Théroigne's cunt, while Bailly fucks Barnave's arse; Lafayette mounts the queen again and gives her another good fuck."

Barnave's arguments in favor of the free expression of the scandal sheets worked within a Rousseauian problematic of the truth. They accepted the scandal sheets' basic principle, which is identity between private and public life (so that if I attack the former, I undermine the latter). Barnave had confidence that truth would triumph in action, in its transparency, its motivations, and in the conscience from which these emanate. Once again we find Rousseau's profound mistrust of any form of mediation, particularly writing.

In her own way, but for different reasons, Marie-Antoinette did not oppose the free expression of the lampoons either; she chose, rather, to ignore them, to remain deaf to their clamor. For as long as possible, complete indifference was her only opposition to the intensity of their cries, to that baroque fury which, through its very clumsiness, at times managed to break new ground.

She mentioned these lampoons to her mother with amusement in a letter of November 30, 1775: "We are in the middle of a satirical song epidemic. They have made some up about everyone at court, men and women alike; French license has even extended to the king. I myself have not been spared. Although this country is fond enough of malice, the songs are so flat and in such bad taste that they are successful neither with the public nor high society."[6]

Marie-Antoinette's failure to recognize the dangers posed by the pamphlets must be attributed to her profound confidence in the world into which she was born — an eventless world, in which time was merely the repetition of ceremony. The Revolution saw time as fluid and driven by events (of which the press made itself both the echo and the engine), in opposition to the ancien régime vision of time as static and immutable.[7] In light of this atemporality, Marie-Antoinette was queen of France by divine right. By birth, she belonged to a history of eternity which decided to ignore all the histories of infamy. The Revolution reinforced the stature of Marie-Antoinette and even exalted her in her sole consideration of eternity.

The queen's mother, Maria Theresa, experienced, politically astute, and conscious of the fragility of the French government and the longstanding hatred between France and Austria, did not share her daughter's serenity. The empress knew that slanderous gossip was a powerful weapon, and she preferred to look it in the face. Satirical songs and lampoons did not amuse her. "Nothing more atrocious has ever been printed," she wrote in August 1774, after receiving, thanks to Beaumarchais (whom she had arrested immediately), a lampoon attacking Marie-Antoinette, entitled *Important Advice for the Spanish Branch on Its Rights to the Crown of France, in the Absence of Heirs, and Which May Be Useful to the Entire Bourbon Family, Especially King Louis XVI.* Thereafter, Maria

Theresa increasingly relied on the comte de Mercy-Argenteau, Austria's ambassador to France and the empress's faithful spy, not only for information on the French government's policies, but on her daughter's every movement as well.

From that point on and for the rest of Maria Theresa's life, a courier left Vienna for Paris (via Brussels) at the beginning of every month. On the 15th of each month, a courier left the court of Versailles with a letter from Marie-Antoinette and two reports from Mercy-Argenteau. The first one, labeled *ostensible*, was a detailed account of Marie-Antoinette's schedule; the second, a secret report reserved for Maria Theresa alone (labeled *tibi soli*), delivered less official information. Marie-Antoinette never suspected this double correspondence and was sometimes stupefied by her mother's clairvoyance, as her mother would sometimes rebuke her by letter, for things Marie-Antoinette thought she alone knew.

Despite her willful indifference, Marie-Antoinette had to face up to the existence of the pamphlets. Like the king and the rest of the royal family, she would find them at Versailles on occasion, or in Paris, at the Opera, for instance. Her equanimity was proportional to the determination of her adversaries. This violence surging up from the outside world did not even touch her when a few days before Marie-Antoinette gave birth to her first son, a wad of manuscripts of songs about her and the other ladies of the court was thrown through the Bull's-Eye.[8] People denied the paternity of the king. As the Goncourts noted, "What outbursts at each pregnancy of the Queen! So many names uttered, even if one counts only the names that are not blasphemous!"[9] Marie-Antoinette did not even deign to look the material over.

Even when thrown by the handful at their targets, the pamphlets failed to rattle the good humor of the queen — thanks, perhaps, to her complete lack of curiosity about the written word.

Reading, an immobile activity demanding sustained concentra-
tion, bored her. It was often said that no one had ever seen her
read a whole book. (But is this because reading disgusted her or
because she did not want to know the ending?) And if she did not
like to read, why should she have forced herself to read material
that insulted, even slandered her? (Her correspondence with her
mother suggests that forcing herself generally was not one of her
strong suits.) While pamphlets have the advantage of being short,
their brevity was offset by their sheer quantity, making the pursuit of lampoonists, during the years they were banned under the
ancien régime, subject to failures of different kinds — though not
due to any lack of perseverance or of repressive measures. "The
police," as Robert Darnton writes, "took the *libelles* seriously,
because they had a serious effect on public opinion, and public
opinion was a powerful force in the declining years of the Old
Regime." The importance of the scandal sheets was all the more
marked, Darnton points out, as "politics took place at court, where
personalities counted more than policies,"[10] and scandal sheets
relied entirely on personal caricature.

Marie-Antoinette's insouciance toward such publications was
linked to her disdainful ignorance of the vague, faceless world
spilling over the fences of the three or four castles in which she
lived. Except for her one-way trip from Vienna to Versailles, she
rarely traveled anywhere in France; she even had to wait three
years to obtain official authorization to leave Versailles just to go
to Paris, although this didn't stop her from going there incognito.
The farthest she ever traveled with her husband was to Reims,
for the king's coronation, and to Varennes, the last leg of the royal
family's disastrous attempt, on June 20, 1791, to escape the Revolution. Louis XVI once went to Normandy, as far as Honfleur.
The king saw the sea ... but the world meant nothing to her.
It only existed in the reduced and miniaturized form of the Petit

Trianon, where she dreamed of recreating the entire universe, and even proposed to reconstruct an erupting volcano.[11]

Marie-Antoinette had nothing to learn from the outside world. The hot-headed, vehement words of the pamphlets were incomprehensible to her and, so, failed to touch her. *The Queen's Reprimand* and other public attacks left her cold. The only advice she listened to came from her mother or from her confessor. Marie-Antoinette did not believe in public opinion. In her eyes, the public wasn't supposed to have an opinion. At best, it enjoyed a role as an extra, which demanded that it disappear offstage, like a good servant, when its presence was no longer required. The four thousand servants at Versailles, who, incidentally, were not regularly paid, were invisible to Marie-Antoinette. When, in 1789, they transformed themselves into spies and even before the royal family was transferred to Paris, held them tight in the vise-grip of an enemy population, the queen must have had the impression of an army springing up out of nowhere.

Contrary to the people who, for years, never stopped fantasizing about her, Marie-Antoinette had no thoughts about the people. At least her indifference guarded her from malevolence; her attitude corresponds to the aristocratic model described by Nietzsche: "[E]ven supposing that the affect of contempt, of looking down from a superior height, *falsifies* the image of that which it despises, it will at any rate still be a much less serious falsification than that perpetrated on its opponent — in *effigy* of course — by the submerged hatred, the vengefulness of the impotent."[12]

The Revolution made the hatred directed at an effigy effective. This sudden realization left Marie-Antoinette baffled. For her, the crowd was a sonorous, euphoric background noise on her first triumphant visits to Paris. When the cheers of rapture died down (silence accompanied her arrival at the meeting of the Estates General in June 1789) or turned into insults (during the

54

painfully slow journey from Versailles to Paris in October 1789), Marie-Antoinette didn't try to interpret the phenomenon. She took fright. That distant entity, the public, generally pitiful and worthy of sympathy and presumed to bear dumb goodwill, was transformed — how was that possible? — into the brutal and vociferous throng swarming around her carriage. They had the voices, the faces, the bodies of another race, a race born of those hordes of the poor, "black with hunger," who, according to the princesse Palatine, had attacked the carriages of the rich in Paris even as early as 1700. Before these starving crowds, galvanized by despair and ready to kill, Marie-Antoinette was overcome with terror. The women called her a tart, the men swore they would kill her. They now had hold of her. She had to make herself equal to their horror.

Catching up with her place in the double logic of the pamphlets, she finally answered with fear and hatred the fear and hatred she inspired as a mythical character. Marie-Antoinette and the people were united by a relationship of reciprocal terror, linked by their fixation on a mutual strangeness amplified to monstrous proportions. They made a somber couple, a composite of obsessive fears and obsessions in which each hallucinated that the other was an awaiting murderer. Pamphlet readers shivered at the representations of the bloodthirsty queen. On her side, the queen felt she was being watched. She imagined a killer behind every door. At night, she would run through the empty, dusty rooms of the Tuileries palace, prey to mounting hatred and terror. She kept mulling over her fury: "This assembly can't be called to account," she wrote to the Count of Fersen on October 31, 1791, "they're a bunch of scoundrels, half-wits and beasts."[13] She dreamed of her revenge: "How happy I will be if, one day, I can be my old self again and prove to those beggars that they didn't fool me!"[14]

To escape the hell of her interminable nights and the scarcely more reassuring days, she eventually longed to be a prisoner. She confided to Mme Campan that she would like to be locked up in a tower by the sea. Princess of the Equinoxes — that would have been a change from the canal of Versailles!

The anonymous voice of the pamphlets never had any effect on Marie-Antoinette. Only one voice had the power of revealing to her that the world was in the process of changing and that things looked bad: the voice of, the profligate and liberal aristocrat, the comte de Mirabeau. He "shouted so loud he frightened Versailles," Céline wrote[15] of the man who triggered Versailles's sudden awakening and the panic that ensued: all those *grandes dames* in flight, decked out as the chambermaids to whom they abandoned their court clothes; counts and marquises dressed up as grooms, donning old costumes from the mascarade room — the Savoyard chimney-sweep or the Ragbag baron, very fashionable for a season. If Mirabeau's voice made the glass panes of the Hall of Mirrors tremble and sent the silhouettes reflected there fleeing, it was not merely because he was exceptionally loud. Although he was a rebel, he was not from the outside; his voice did not offend with any vulgar accent. Mirabeau spoke the language of the aristocracy. Even if he contested it, he belonged to this sect, the club, and not to the undifferentiated world, without right of access, of the plebian. His was a voice the aristocracy could not ignore.

With a genius for betrayal and irrepressible transgressive strength, Mirabeau knew equally well the two camps facing each other; he knew, in particular, how divided the French were even before they had formed opposing camps. And it was the spirit of division, not the camp spirit, that interested him. Thanks to his deceitful qualities, Mirabeau the orator had no trouble finding the right words to impress the royal family; and while the orator was talking, Mirabeau the libertine let himself be seduced by the beauty of the queen. But she couldn't look at him without fear and loathing. Perhaps she had read his libertine writings (though not all the way through!).

If she didn't trust dangerous personalities, it was because she had no experience of danger — except for gambling, and even then, she knew her heaviest debts would be forgiven by her husband, merely requiring an increase in the allowance earmarked for the queen's expenses. She was in no danger of sharing the fate of Casanova's gambler — Casanova himself, perhaps — who, after losing everything one night, left at dawn, in silk stockings and an embroidered gilet, entrusting to Casanova his pregnant young wife and the new name he had just chosen to carry on his adventures. He took the road east... After a night of rotten luck, Marie-Antoinette fell asleep without too much tossing and turning...

Mirabeau's intelligence alone sufficed to make him a dangerous character in Marie-Antoinette's eyes. Devoid of any intellectual inclination, she found demonstrative, energetic, cultivated intelligence threatening. Far from exciting her, the prospect of meeting such people discouraged, even intimidated her. She wouldn't rule out the idea of conversing with Voltaire, but anxiously asked what to say. As for wit, she only liked society repartee — quick and fluid, passing time and causing laughter — in which talking was as intoxicating as dancing or ice skating. According to Talleyrand (whose career went from Bishop of Autun to foreign minister under Napoleon), his mother was the very model of the art of conversation, which combined the brilliant and the evanescent. She systematically avoided *bons mots*, pauses in the airy movement of speech. "*Bons mots* are remembered, and she wanted only to please and to let her words be forgotten."[16]

Mme de Lamballe, perhaps incapable of verbal seduction, took to its logical conclusion the wish that "her words be forgotten." She was unequalled in the play of absences. "She never had an opinion of her own; in conversation she always adopted the opinion of the person who passed for the wittiest, in a way that was entirely unique. Whenever there was a serious discussion, she never spoke, pretending to fall into a trance; then she would suddenly appear to snap out of her reverie and repeat, word for word, as though it came from her, what the person whose opinion she had decided to adopt had just said. She affected great surprise when told someone had just said the same thing; she assured everyone she hadn't heard it."[17] She spoke as if she were swooning.

Marie-Antoinette enjoyed the company of the princesse de Lamballe and Mme de Polignac precisely because they were not women of wit; their company was pleasant and amusing and protected her from the inhospitable spaces opened up by bitter reflection or flights of abstraction. She did not like Mirabeau because his talk was a breach in the strict boundaries of courtly conversation. The unbridled energy and interpellatory violence of revolutionary oratory must have been shocking to people trained according to the principles of jesuitical rhetoric, for whom power was, by definition, silent: the power of kings, like that of the gods, expressed itself entirely in the radiant splendor of their appearance. Even if Mirabeau was at pains to cover up his oratorical boldness, words, rhythms, and intonations surged forth that had never before been heard at Versailles, except under cover of theatrical license. Mirabeau's speech was even harder to take because, in bringing the reality of the Revolution to Versailles, it merely confirmed the distant omen expressed by Maria Theresa in a letter to her daughter ten years earlier: "The future is not bright."

Mirabeau managed to pull off a coup unique among the leading political actors of the day by dying a natural death, on April 2, 1791, right in the middle of all the revolutionary tumult. The announcement of his death was immediately followed by rumors accusing Marie-Antoinette of poisoning him. As one pamphlet put it: "I'd tell all.... I'd say thousands of men were dispatched by her own hand once they had served her pleasure.... I'd say that, despite her aversion to national dress, she didn't hesitate to grant her favors to General Mothier [marquis de Lafayette].... I'd say the poison that killed Mirabeau was distilled in her own mortar. I'd say only her murderous insinuations could corrupt the good nature of the weakest of kings.... I'd say...all our calamities, past, present, and to come, have always been and will always be her doing."[18]

The Pamphlet's Murderous Vocation

The aim of Mirabeau's tortuous maneuvers was to obtain gold for himself. For his royal interlocutors, apart from the chance to broaden their view of the world and enrich their vocabulary with new words, dealing with Mirabeau represented the possibility of surviving the Revolution unscathed and even of holding on to power. Unless, that is, he were to produce the opposite effect, his thundering voice merely exacerbating the court's panic. Should that be the case, he would only have brought the court closer to the threats suspended in the literature of the pamphlets, those deadly arrows buried in the virulent prose and nasty verses. For the pamphlets, between the attacks they formulate and their designated victim, trace the outline of a suspended sentence. Their aim is to put their characters to death. Their entirely negative heroes, vicious by vocation and application, never for a second stop wanting to do wrong. By dint of their conscientiousness, these villains lose all sense of the degrees of evil. Louise Robert, in her long pamphlet *The Crimes of the Queens of France from the Beginning of the Monarchy until Marie-Antoinette* (1791) — a text bristling with stupidity and misogyny — cited the example of the ferocious queen Fredegond, murderer of her husband and "executioner of humankind," for whom crime is a need. One day, for example, Fredegond offers jewels and fabrics to her daughter Rigont, who bends over the coffer where the presents are kept. "And then," Robert writes, "that unnatural mother shut the lid on her head."

In *A Conference Between Mme de Polignac and Mme de La Motte in Saint James Park,* Mme de Polignac, "that female chameleon," turned up as the "banished favorite," anxious to renounce her former mistress and to win the friendship of Mme de La Motte. But the inflexible La Motte shows "the idol of Versailles" perfect contempt, rejecting her advances with a line from tragedy: "Adieu, Madame, go and live in obscurity, if you can enjoy such happiness." This of course reeks of perfidiousness since everyone knows there is not a crime that Mme de Polignac hasn't had a hand in, that when she isn't sinking her teeth into men, she's taking it out on animals. "'As for us,' she shrieks with a laugh, which, dear reader, you must compare the highest note of the most satanic soprano, 'as though our evil genius could never fail us, being unable to do any more harm to men, we wore horses to death along the way.'"[19]

If the Messalina Polignac was capable of such excesses, it would be unthinkable for the Messalina Marie-Antoinette to let her favorite outdo her. She who lives only for murder and dirty deeds, who can extend the effects of her cruelty over a whole population, was hardly going to balk at minor misdemeanors. The pamphlet *Tel gens tel encens* added a novel twist to the litany of the perverse queen's crimes: the "royal spit": "While citizens were rushing to gather all the trimmings she could want for her spouse's new palace... the spiteful woman commits public outrage against us, infuriating citizens with her contempt.... In full view of one French citizen, she allows her aversion to explode, and ends up spitting on him as incontestable proof of the hatred she has sworn us. This last stroke of malevolence was recently committed in the Tuileries, as she emerged from one of those filthy orgies that she has so blithely offered us."[20]

The pamphlets reported scandalous events that reveal the exclusively harmful nature of the characters presented. Reading or declaiming these texts was a call to insurrection: we've allowed ourselves to be spat on long enough! The symbolic violence of the pamphlets cried out to be made real by action. The lampoon tended to meet its target, to blaze with it in the same destructive rage. Identification between the textual and the real character was more or less direct and concrete. It was made in several ways, for example, through the doubling effect of an effigy. On September 21, 1787, during the parliamentary riots, antiroyalist pamphlets were distributed and joyful bonfires lit; an effigy of the duchesse de Polignac was burned. Alternatively, that identification was made through an intermediary: a newspaper reported that one of Lafayette's guards was found assassinated by a dagger; the handle of the dagger was wrapped in a bloodstained scandal sheet, on which the words "Go and prepare for your master's arrival" were written. Finally, the identification was made directly, at the very scene of punishment: On his trip to the scaffold, the condemned would see copies of his "private life" or some other biographical lampoon being handed out, explaining how he came to be there. Certain anecdotes became refrains sung in chorus. The condemned sometimes had the bitter experience of recognizing his own words sung by the crowd, as with "Give Gorsas Back His Shirts," which accompanied the unfortunate journalist to the guillotine. This absurd song was put together from lines Gorsas had written when the king's aunts fled into exile.

Under her window at Sainte-Pélagie prison, Mme Roland heard shouted the insults that the radical journalist Hébert let fly in his *Père Duchesne*. She complained of being treated even worse than the queen whom she detested. She would have been outraged had she known that, after her execution, an article in the *Moniteur universel* would link her with Marie-Antoinette and Olympe de Gouges in the same attack, that beyond personal and political differences, she would be placed in the broader category of un-natural women: "The tribunal soon set women a good example, which will no doubt not be lost on them, for justice, ever impartial, always combines severity with a lesson. Marie-Antoinette... was a bad mother and a debauched wife, and she died weighed down by the imprecations of those whose ruin she would have liked to have achieved.... The Roland woman, with her fine mind and grand ambitions, philosopher of the short note, queen for a day... was a monster in all her dealings...."[21]

Degrees of Punishment

When Mme Roland was confronted by the pamphlets sung to her from the other side of the bars, she realized that the "lesson" they implied could not be far off. At Versailles, when Marie-Antoinette heard people talking about the pamphlets attacking her, she imagined she could ignore them, remain deaf to the threats they contained. Surrounded by close friends (who thought only of exploiting her favors) she would try to preserve a universe closed to the outside world, a tiny oasis of sweetness and light, sheltered by screens with painted roses, a refuge in white linen and pastel grays. Here, walled off from the vitriol surrounding her, she composed and sang:

> *Ah! if in your village there is*
> *A gentle and charming shepherd*
> *One cherishes at first sight*
> *And loves even more after that,*
> *He is my friend, give him back to me.*

I have his love, he has my trust
I have his love, he has my trust.

If the notes of his oboe
Make the shepherdess wonder,
If his sweet plaintive voice
Charms the echo of your woods,
He is my friend, give him back to me.
I have his love, he has my trust
I have his love, he has my trust...

Marie-Antoinette's blind behavior toward the hostility of the court and the commoners intensified her isolation and redoubled her foreign status, which had stigmatized her from the moment she set foot on French soil.

The first lampoons, which were the court's work, were meant to provoke her repudiation of the throne. Her departure would have satisfied numerous parties. First, that of the comte de Provence, one of Louis XVI's younger brothers, who found coming second intolerable. The day after Louis XVI's coronation, he confided his exasperation to prince de Montbarey: "Look at me, condemned for life never to act as I should like, for from now on my duty is to always put my foot wherever the king, my brother, has just lifted his." Perhaps to attenuate the resentment of his brothers (while the comte de Provence slyly hated yet respected form, the youngest brother, the comte d'Artois, was simply violently disrespectful), the king relaxed protocol and permitted his brothers and sisters-in-law to forego using the obligatory title "Majesty" and employing the third person pronoun when addressing him.[22] This was a significant change in a society whose whole ethic rested on fastidious respect for the hierarchies of birth, a society where the individual existed only through submission to etiquette.

"One no longer has a clue who one is," the princesse Palatine exclaimed in the final years of Louis XIV's long reign, bewildered by the vulgarity of young people who could remain sprawled on a divan in the presence of a blue-blooded princess.

The king's relaxation of family protocol did not succeed for a second in dispelling the discontent and ambition of the comte de Provence. It was, after all, just another order from the king! In 1773, only three years after Marie-Antoinette's arrival at Versailles, the empress Maria Theresa wrote: "That prince seems false to me and may be a spy for the ruling party."[23] The comte de Provence could no longer disguise his "falseness" when, in 1778, the queen's first child, Marie Thérèse Charlotte, was born. After her birth, the tone of the pamphlets became much more aggressive, and still more violent in 1781, when Marie-Antoinette brought a son into the world. The comte de Provence was suspected not only of taking part in the slander campaign but of instigating it. What is known, in any case, is that he wrote material satirizing the royal couple. According to writer and journalist Louis-Sébastien Mercier, his contemporary, the comte de Provence composed noëls (satirical songs sung to the tune of a Christmas carol) and other songs attacking his brother the king. It became fashionable at court to mock Louis XVI. "In no reign," Mercier notes, "was the talent for the epigram against the person of the prince brought to such a high degree of perfection."[24] When, after seven years, Marie-Antoinette became a mother, the attacks returned to the theme of her infidelity, which had previously been denounced in a pamphlet of 1774 (cited above), famous among Parisians and in courts abroad, entitled Important Advice for the Spanish Branch on Its Rights to the Crown of France, in the Absence of Heirs, and Which May Be Useful to the Entire Bourbon Family, Especially King Louis XVI.

In the pamphlets, the paternity of the queen's children was more often than not attributed to comte d'Artois. "Now I am stuck for nine months, thanks to your gaff," she says to him in one pamphlet, with her usual flippancy! Another text has the queen inform the reader of Artois's reaction to paternity: "I soon realized what an unnatural character he was, when I told the adorable prince, 'Ah! dear Artois, your little dauphin [...] is kicking me in the stomach.' 'And me in the ass, my darling,' he replied. 'but f*** it! Have patience, we'll manage to get rid of it like all the rest.'"[25]

Life at Versailles and relations between members of the royal family, as caricatured in the pamphlets, are reminiscent of the orgy scenes in certain films of Erich von Stroheim. In *Queen Kelly* (1928), for example, Stroheim exalted the depravity of the Old World and the ancien régime. Through his gold-rimmed monocle, or behind the camera lens, his eye focuses on tableaux of debauchery. These are set against a backdrop of palaces draped in heavy crimson, or in enchanted parks, under showers of flower petals. Kings and queens crawl on all fours as far as their canopy beds, where they collapse dead drunk on satin pillows. They don't have the strength to straighten their cockeyed crowns on their drunken heads; they have only enough energy to drain the last bottle of champagne, while dealing their prisoners a few casual blows. The king falls asleep, snoring like an animal. The utterly depraved and insatiable queen takes the whip to innocent young girls who hurtle down immense staircases, completely naked, under the implacable gaze of the guards. So this is how one lives when one can get away with murder — by definition, the privilege of the great. The voice of the public, necessarily moral, is unanimous: "Trollop queens have always wreaked havoc."

The denunciation of the queen by the court and the king's next of kin served the fratricidal battle that the comte de Provence was waging against his elder brother, destroying any possibility of unity not only among the nobility (annihilated as a

political class by Louis XIV), but also within the royal family. From
the point of view of the comte de Provence's destiny, the Revolution and the death of Louis XVI, followed by the long Napoleonic
reign, were merely detours necessary for him to realize his stubborn desire to reign. Louis Massignon sums it up in his usual suc-
cinct style: "Provence: determined to reign at whatever cost;
afflicted with the congenital complex of Cain, which will make of
him, through jealousy, the most oblivious and the most successful
of regicides."[26]

After all the years of waiting and exile, in 1815 the comte de
Provence became Louis XVIII; he finally managed to place his
foot where he was the *first* to tread. But by then, suffering from
dropsy and obesity, he had considerable trouble putting one foot
in front of the other. The incurable disappointment, the wound
that never heals, was not the frustration of unfulfilled desire (a
fever that can be exciting): it began with the fulfillment of desire,
now indistinguishable from reality.

The queen's repudiation would have delighted the comte de
Provence. It would not have unduly upset Adélaïde, Victoire,
and Sophie, the daughters of Louis XV (Louis XVI's aunts),
who conducted "a war of intrigue and sarcasm that went along
with that of Monsieur (the comte de Provence)"[27] against Marie-
Antoinette. Their sister, Mme Louise, had taken the veil at the
Carmelite convent of Saint-Denis. (Going by her last words, she
would have been completely detached from worldly intrigue.
According to Mme Campan, who claimed to have heard it from
Louis XVI, Mme Louise died uttering a command: "To heaven,
and be quick about it!") Louis XVI was very fond of his aunts; he
treated them far better than Louis XV ever did. Adélaïde, Victoire, and Sophie had long since seen better days by the time the
dauphine arrived, a happy adolescent, always laughing, delighting

in conversation and children and trying in vain to win the old ladies' friendship.

Adélaïde, Victoire, and Sophie never married. They lived at court and were especially interested in observing the honors and precedence owed to them. Their only perspective on love was a visit — punctual but rushed — from their "beloved" libertine father, who was always in the clutches of his latest favorite. Thus abandoned, the ladies sought refuge among the confessors to whom they whispered their all too rare sins. The "pretty pack of abbots and vicars," as the Goncourts called them, found in Mesdames their most steady clients. None of this makes for loveable natures; they were, in fact, surly censors who found the dauphine's mistakes in French no laughing matter (their superiority in this respect, at least, was indisputable). As Mme Campan, who knew them well, having read to them before being appointed Marie-Antoinette's first chambermaid, wrote: "If Mesdames had not imposed a large number of chores upon themselves, they would have been very much to be pitied."[28]

One of the numerous chores that only just saved Mesdames from being in the unhappy women category was scandalmongering. Spinners of Boredom and Guardians of Etiquette, the Three Fates let her have it as soon as the young lady turned her back. They did their utmost to see that the court was in league against her and even staged feuds among themselves. "I know that Mme Adélaïde and Mme Sophie were busy for a long time trying to turn the archduchesse against Mme Victoire, who is unquestionably the nicest of the three sisters and the one with the most character," noted Mercy-Argenteau, who, unquestionably, never missed a trick.[29]

Mesdames' opposition to Marie-Antoinette was not only personal. They were adherents of the "French Party," which stood in opposition to the party of the foreign minister, the duc de Choiseul, a partisan of alliance with Austria and the man responsible for Louis XVI's marriage to Marie-Antoinette, which was preceded by years of negotiating. Marie-Antoinette arrived in France as a hostage from France's traditional enemy. Her presence overstimulated the spirit of conspiracy reigning at Versailles. Perceived as the enemy, she did not enjoy the support of her husband, who was, at first, entirely under Mesdames' influence. Marie-Antoinette's only ally and supporter, the duc de Choiseul was disgraced in 1770, only months after her arrival in France. The empress Maria Theresa was saddened by the exit from the French political stage of the man with whom she had concluded the Franco-Austrian rapprochement, of which Marie-Antoinette was the pledge. And Marie-Antoinette felt the concrete effects of a loss that deprived her of protection from the combined hatred of the comte de Provence, Mesdames' party, and the entire court nobility dedicated to the pursuit of an anti-Austrian policy. *For what she represented* (an obstacle to the king's brother's desire to reign and the triumph of the diplomatic strategy of the former minister Choiseul), Marie-Antoinette very quickly became a prime target for the royalist scandal sheets. She was, structurally, the enemy to be destroyed.

On this level, the antiroyalist pamphlets took up where the royalist pamphlets left off. Marie-Antoinette remained the heroine of crime, but now she threatened not the honor of royalty, but the honor, the very existence, of the nation. The antiroyalist pamphlets used the same themes; they merely amplified them. Like the royalist pamphlets, they demanded the queen's removal and separation from Louis XVI. Since the queen was solely responsible for France's woes and royal mismanagement, her disappearance would suffice to make the French happy again.

At first the revolutionary pamphlets were content to demand that the queen be removed and locked up in a convent. But such a punishment would not have been very spectacular. It would even have meant the end of the spectacle, which is why, as a consolation for the exit of such a fascinating, irreplaceable performer, certain pamphlets insisted that the queen's elimination should be preceded by a public confession, as the satirical *Testament of Marie-Antoinette of Austria* put it: "I beg my husband and the nation to grant me pardon for all my sins, which I have already partly revealed in a confession made public, printed, and distributed at the beginning of the month."[30] (In the pamphlets, the substitution of the first person for the third did not introduce any subjective element, any depth or complexity of identity. By design it must not incline the reader to sympathize. Vertigo or fusion with the person saying "I" — effects of reading autobiographical texts — were ruled out. When Marie-Antoinette expressed herself in the first person in a pamphlet in which she has a speaking role, she was merely internalizing a sanction, identifying herself with an external image. It was the voice of the people speaking through her.)

A lampoon against the princesse Polignac expressed a like desire for her public humiliation before the cheated and offended people: "Yes, Madame, you must do penance, and as the choice is up to the confessor, here is the penance I impose in the name of the nation. Shave your head, don a gray hessian dress as your only adornment, and go to the august assembly of the Estates General in this garb to make atonement and deliver up any remains of your plundering."[31] Images of women as repentant sinners, offered up to public condemnation and pardon as they had once prostituted themselves to lewdness, exceeded the dry demands of justice. It was as Mary Magdalens bathed in tears, and not as political criminals, that the queen and her cronies were judged in fantasy. Marie-Antoinette the fallen queen had to be as conspicuous, as much on parade, as Marie-Antoinette the triumphant queen. She had to be seen wearing the attributes of her decline as sumptuously and luxuriously as she had sported the attributes of her impunity (hence the general frustration at her trial and condemnation). The great scenes of repentance essential to the medieval tradition, in which religious and civil justice were indissociable, continually haunted the judicial imagination of the Revolution. Marie-Antoinette, condemned, should have behaved, by way of expiation, with the same magnificence as Gilles de Rais; she should have gotten down on her knees as he had and begged the people for forgiveness. The monstrosity of one's crimes was thus proportionate to the nobility of one's birth. The judges were linked to the condemned by a bond of compassion. Putting the guilty person to death took on the value of a sacrificial rite. This ceremony of expiation was only possible on the basis of religious communion, or at least recognition of a common humanity.

But the more hatred of the queen grew, the more the possibility of any connection with her was excluded — whether she was being reviled or atoning for her sins. The unity of the people was indeed consolidated by this exclusion; the new fraternity fed off it. There was no longer any question of complicity between the judges and the guilty party. "She who does not mind prostituting lilies" was no longer exhorted to confess her crimes. Her confession would no longer be considered valid. She was no longer expected to return to virtue. *The Queen's Reprimand,* a pamphlet of 1789, still cautioned: "Resplendent Queen, profit at last from your woes by repenting of your wicked deeds; consider the fact that wrinkles of debauchery are already overtaking your beautiful features." But the tone of the pamphlets hardened very swiftly. Punitive measures — that is, letting the queen live, but *punishing her* — which implicitly treat the queen as a penitent, were no longer prescribed. Marie-Antoinette, a hardened criminal whose treacherous soul even led her to fake remorse, deserved death. "I see the fatal tool! ... It awaits me," she groaned in *The Great Disease of Marie-Antoinette.*

The egalitarian and mechanical death of the guillotine did not allow messages from the beyond. The corpse of the condemned radiated no halo of mystery and malediction. This end without agony or omen was the opposite of the death of witches, those female poisoners and magicians who, in the convulsions wrung from them as they burn at the stake, continued to enthrall their audience. Thus, the guillotine was the perfect instrument for putting an end to the perverse influence of an infernal creature such as Marie-Antoinette. But did it really succeed?

Considering the inhuman crimes ascribed to her, the guillotine, some thought, would be too much of an honor to bestow on Marie-Antoinette. To them, her death should partake of the same bestial confusion as her "foul orgies." The savagery of a quarry's death in hunting scenes would suit the bacchanalian queen better than the guillotine's precision: "Monster in every way, one cannot look at you without trembling or imagine you without thinking of Jezebel.... There is no Jehovah to sacrifice you to, we despise you too much ... but there are dogs to feast on your corpse.... They are waiting for you."[32] The Montagnard Hébertist and "violent dechristianizer" Lequinio, who doubtless considered the death penalty too quick a punishment, proposed that Louis XVI be sent to jail or to the galleys.[33] As for Marie-Antoinette, she should be forced to sweep the streets of Paris or be taken on as a worker at the Salpêtrière hospital.

Marie-Antoinette delivered up to the silence of the convent, to public prosecution and conviction, to sweeping the streets of Paris, or to the dogs — such were the permutations of her hallucinated and exaggerated torture and execution. She only perceived them in the final moments, when public opinion had assumed full reign and was stamping its decrees with the seal of truth, when a pamphleteer could declare, without eliciting the slightest doubt, "I shall tell all," and then cobble together every crime that came

71

into his head. At that point Marie-Antoinette felt no desire to belittle the platitudes and stylistic poverty of the scandal sheets. She was at their mercy. She now had to take them seriously. This almost transitionless shift from indifference to fright precluded any strategic position for her. By the time Marie-Antoinette emerged from her serenity, she had become the prey and the incarnation of a language of fantasy, whose political reach was beyond her ken. The word of the pamphlets had become flesh, and this flesh was her very self.

Had she read in *The Testament of Marie-Antoinette* "When one is as guilty as I am, public vengeance should hasten my end," she could not have distanced herself from the sentence the lampoonist put in her mouth, nor could she have deflected the mortal consequences of her assimilation to this mythical monster who, for years, had been mobilizing the hostility of the people toward the government. She had become "the scourge devastating France," the ogress of Trianon. Just after her death in October 1793, a pamphlet was published entitled *The Testament of Marie-Antoinette, the Widow Capet*. It opened with the words: "Frenchmen, Republicans [....] You have purged the earth of a monster who was its abomination!"[34] The new world could not be born without her dying.

Marie-Antoinette was the victim of ideological inflation systematically fueled by the pamphlets and the press. Her immediate, intuitive, seductive conduct sprang from a state of mind appropriate to the secure world of inherited power. She had no other survival skills beyond the manipulation of courtiers and the strategic coldness that accompanied it.

Marie-Antoinette and Talleyrand:
The Actress and the Master of Ceremonies

> Talleyrand's function was first of all that of master of
> ceremonies — in a period that had forgotten what cere-
> monies meant and therefore claimed to get along with-
> out them, though it slid back clumsily at every step.
> — Roberto Calasso[35]

Charles-Maurice de Talleyrand-Périgord (1754–1838) had the great talent of deflecting from himself the rage for vengeance that powered the revolutions. Far from being seen as a man from the appalling past, he appeared again and again as the man necessary to the *new* government — as much during the Revolution as under the Directory, the Empire, and the Restoration, up until the bourgeois reign of Louis Philippe. Talleyrand began his long career under the prevailing impiety, accepting the ecclesiastic path in obedience to family authority, but without feigning a hint of vocation. In 1788, he was appointed bishop of Autun by Louis XVI, who, out of genuine piety, was personally opposed to the decision.

Representing the clergy in the Estates General, Talleyrand celebrated mass at the Champ de Mars to commemorate national federation on July 14, 1790. In driving rain that failed to dampen the enthusiasm of the federated, Talleyrand, the impious mediator, officiated between two opposing beliefs: that of the people, who had come from every province of France, united in this "vast farandole" sung by the historian Jules Michelet; and that of the king and queen, outsiders as far as passion for the new religion went and anchored in the dogma of royalty by divine right. The king delivered a sermon, halfheartedly; the queen dreamed of hearing mass somewhere else. She remained rigid within an atmosphere of joyful, gentle camaraderie, unable to imagine joining

73

in the fun, wanting only to flee the festivities and their, for her, threatening obverse. "And you, Madame," apostrophized Michelet (who might have adopted Henri Michaux's phrase for the occasion: "I am speaking to the beheaded!"), "this childlike people, so confident, so blind, dancing with such insouciance a moment ago, between their sad past and their formidable future — don't you feel sorry for them?... Why that dubious light in your beautiful blue eyes? One royalist noticed it: 'Look at the magician,' said the comte de Virieu...."[36] The "magician" would give anything to get out of such a tight spot while Talleyrand, at the altar, accomplished the ritual gestures with all due respect.

When Bonaparte was presented to the Directory in 1795, he was greeted by Talleyrand who, Chateaubriand wrote, "received the conqueror at the altar, recalling having once said mass at quite a different altar."[37] From one altar to the next, one conqueror to the next, Talleyrand carved out an unparalleled diplomatic career. He was the minister of foreign affairs under the Directory, Napoleon, and Louis XVIII and returned after a brief eclipse under Charles X (1824–1830), as ambassador to London under Louis Philippe. This surprising flexibility, which allowed him not only to glide through political upheavals unscathed but to occupy in each successive regime a post of the first order, has often been interpreted as evidence of a colossal capacity for treachery. Betrayal is seen as Talleyrand's sole vocation: his permanence from one government to the next thus seems a sure sign of his corruption. This is certainly the way it looked to Chateaubriand, who concluded that the illusion of a return to royalty was being created when he saw that the first politician Louis XVIII met with on his return from the Hundred Days was Talleyrand: "Suddenly a door opens: Vice enters silently on the arm of Crime, M. Talleyrand supported by M. Fouché; the infernal vision passes slowly before me, goes into the king's chambers and disappears. Fouché had come to swear faith and allegiance to his lord; the loyal regicide, on his knees, placed the hands that felled Louis XVI's head in the hands of the martyred king's brother; the bishop apostate was guarantor for the oath."[38]

Virtue, as represented by Chateaubriand, is not silent. It sallies forth, alone, and exhausts itself in declarations, admonitions, open letters, calls to remain faithful to principles. Chateaubriand's political career, unlike that of Talleyrand, whom he detested, was remarkable for its discontinuity. The high points — those Chateaubriand himself glorified the most — were resignations (following the assassination of the duc d'Enghien, for which, as we know, Talleyrand was partly responsible); expulsions (appointed minister of foreign affairs by Louis XVIII in December 1822, Chateaubriand was dismissed six months later); and exiles. Virtue talks out loud and averts its gaze, outraged at the frightful interlacing of Vice and Crime. Vice (in the person of Talleyrand) encapsulates apostasy, seething with repudiations. He covered his tracks, leaving few traces, only to have built, in the shadows, a vast memorial to the unsaid.

No doubt Talleyrand was extremely adept at secrecy and betrayal, but his genius was accompanied by a fidelity of sorts (which, on the one hand, makes him even more diabolical and, on the other, accounts for his success): attachment not to any particular content but to a style. For Talleyrand, *savoir-faire* counted more than facts, and merit accrued to the official signatories rather than the actual authors. As Roberto Calasso writes in *The Ruin of Kasch*, a text so acute and original as to constitute in itself an homage to the princely spirit, Talleyrand was "the only person who has managed to betray everything, with the exception of style."[39] This flair, which has been lost over the centuries, made Talleyrand indispensable to every brand of politics. Style has no object or privileged situation; its strength lies in enabling one to deal with anyone, under any circumstance. Talleyrand was a good listener, good at decoding, good at hearing and commanding several registers at once and working a connection precisely between those that seemed the most incompatible. His was the art of nuance, of the unexpected smile, of detachment.

Talleyrand's intelligence matched foresight with the reserve of a defensive strategy. The discipline of staying in power implies constant attention to any manifestation of public opinion, so it is not surprising that Talleyrand read the pamphlets, as much for his amusement as for information. He followed the pamphlets' verbal extravagances closely, those continual calls to insurrection which, while denouncing abuse, permitted themselves every verbal abuse imaginable. Marie-Antoinette had long misread such excesses as merely ridiculous, as confused and eminently forgettable drivel, then suddenly discovered that these slanders set to verse were also concrete threats. But Talleyrand had from the start seen their conventions of style as a political tactic. He was therefore in a position to guess their effect and have a hand in their elaboration.

The 105 pamphlets that were part of Talleyrand's library are now housed in the New York Public Library, which acquired them in 1937. They are mainly concerned with finance and the clergy. Hardly any are about the queen; the odd one deals with Mme de Polignac, focusing on "all the finer points of her cunt's gymnastics." The titles themselves speak volumes: *The Inside-out Skullcap*, by the author of *I Don't Give a Damn*; *A New Hymn*; *The Passions of Our Venerable Clergy, According to Today's Gospel*; *The Monk Who Is No Fool, at the Estates General*; *Confession and Repentance of Mme de P[olignac], or The New Magdalen Converted*; *The Confessions of Marie-Antoinette, Former Queen of France*; *Petition of Women for Admission to the Estates General* (wherein they suggest: "Shouldn't they send us as ambassadors?"); *Letter from a Woman in Childbirth to Beaumarchais*; *Ah! Ah! Conversation on Current Affairs between a Royalist and a Member of Parliament*; *Rape*, by abbé Maury (which contains such clever repartee as: "Ah! he's killing me, the rogue, the monster / Good, good, Madame, insults excite me"); and so on.

The pamphlets open the floodgates of caricature, overturning all dogma and joining in the background of raillery and insolence against which, for Talleyrand, the world was defined. They offer the possibility of ironic distance but are also valuable as warning and instruction, for the rhetorical turgidity of the pamphlets was, for Talleyrand, a dissuasive tool as far as the temptation of allegiance goes. He saw in the extravagance of their language a formal purulence, a playful mask. And he stuck to the same practices of demystification when confronted by the period of overhaul inaugurated by the fall of royalty. Talleyrand understood that political intelligence "would not be to impede or foster those convulsions (cruel childishness in either case), but rather to *soften the blow*, to coat the sharp edges in sweet essence of balm, to wrap them in noble gauze that had been abandoned in attics! And above all to dissociate those convulsions from *faith*: to refuse to credit them with that *extra something* which they always claim to represent."[40]

Reading the pamphlets, Talleyrand confirmed his systematic practice of deflating moral values — in keeping with the incredulity that characterized his whole enterprise. Master of ceremonies for the advance of modern history, Talleyrand's official presentation of events was accompanied, quietly, by a satanic snigger.

His role as master of ceremonies became more and more necessary the further the politesse of the ancien régime faded from memory. His "grand style" was called on to fill in the gaps. "Everyone dreamed of the Court, but memories of the proper gestures were already beginning to fade."[41]

Marie-Antoinette was the proper gesture incarnate. She lent her glow to the court's final representations, in which she played the lead.

Politician of the morning after, Talleyrand worked with time. Marie-Antoinette, on the contrary, is an arrested image.

From the fashion plate to the profile of the woman condemned: one woman's story, the end of a world.

CHAPTER THREE

Queen of Fashion

> The Tuileries Palace, a large jail filled with the con-
> demned, stood amid the celebration of destruction.
> Those sentenced also amused themselves as they
> waited for the *cart*, the *clipping*, and the *red shirt* they
> had put out to dry, and through the windows the
> Queen's circle could be seen, stunningly illuminated.
> — Chateaubriand, *Mémoires d'outre-tombe*[1]

Good and Beautiful

The fixed image we have of Marie-Antoinette, set in the diamond
sparkle of her youth and grace, is a consequence of her execution.
The guillotine made of her, in our collective memory, the last
queen, *The* Queen. But fascination with the queen's image was not
only a posthumous phenomenon. Even during her lifetime, a powerful ambivalence was felt toward her, provoking desire and hatred
and a confusion between fantasy and fact. Marie-Antoinette's al-
lure, analogous to that of twentieth-century movie stars, had its
source in the queen's private passion for glamour.

Marie-Antoinette lived in the emotion of her beauty. Her
aesthetic sense, even her ethics, were indissociable from that
rapture. She knew what suited her. Trianon was decorated and

furnished with the same sense of color and harmony that Marie-Antoinette observed in choosing her robes. The queen loved her beauty, and this love affected everyone. Her self-satisfaction did not wane even at the peak of her unpopularity, when she was the first to recognize that "the time for illusions is over."[2] She attracted strangers — people who had just arrived in Paris, those curious about the Revolution. Gouverneur Morris, coming to Paris from America in 1789, was in a hurry to visit Versailles: "The King is well lodged," he notes in his diary. "The Queen's appartments [sic] I cannot see because her Majesty is there, and yet 'tis ten to one but I should like her better than any other Part of the furniture. Her Picture, however, by Madame Lebrun, will do as well and perhaps better for it is very beautiful. Doubtless as much so as the original."[3] (The original pleased him so much, in fact, that he later tried to hatch a plan of escape for the queen.)

If Marie-Antoinette rejected or ignored the sublime image of royalty in order to obtain personal satisfaction, it was not out of antipathy to the world of representation. Unlike Louis XVI, she adored and excelled in that world. But she was first and foremost sensitive to her own pleasure, and the abstract ideal of sovereignty — as understood by Louis XIV and her mother, the empress, who tried in vain to inculcate it in her — did nothing for her. Marie-Antoinette shrank the powers of appearance to the narrow sphere of a family theater. She abandoned the ceremony of Versailles, where effects are always at one remove and rigorously predictable, for the cosy utopia of Trianon, a place where she could enjoy being herself under the close gaze of the chosen few who constituted her society. At Versailles, out of respect for etiquette, "court society carried out a representation of itself."[4] By playing their roles there, the king and queen maintained the symbolism of a hierarchy. But at Trianon, abandoning all etiquette, Marie-Antoinette restricted the circle of narcissism to her own

person. It was no longer the glamour of a caste being staged, but
that of a woman — one fleeing the boredom and immoderation of
Versailles and taking refuge in herself, by the pond or in the *salle
des Fraîcheurs*. Everything that came near Marie-Antoinette irradi-
ated the seductiveness proper to her person. She inhabited a living, vibrant, musical, lovable space. But outside the sphere of her
seduction, she preferred to be as absent as possible, evading the
profession of queen when it demanded of her (and this is the only
thing it did demand) detachment, indifference, the mechanical
performance of a function. Some days after he visited the royal
apartments, Morris was invited by Mme de Montboissier for a
stroll in the gardens of the Petit Trianon. He rightly remarked,
"Royalty has here endeavored, at great Expense to conceal itself from its own Eye but the Attempt is vain."[5] In this spirit of
side-stepping the starchy ritual and gravity of Versailles, Marie-
Antoinette and her friends abandoned themselves, for a time, to a
craze for little games. They kept themselves amused with blind
man's bluff, riddles, and especially *descampativos*, a game that in-
volves playing the king. At the end of his reign, Louis XIV himself
had yielded to the whimsical charm of the young duchesse de
Bourgogne, dauphine and wife of Louis de France, the king's
son. The king was enchanted, along with Mme de Maintenon
(the canny young duchess had understood it was no use getting
on with one without the other), with the innumerable caprices the
duchess dreamed up and immediately put into action in contempt
of all protocol. When riding in a carriage, the duchesse de Bourgogne, "cannot sit still for a second; she darts from one corner to
the other, jigging about like a little monkey."[6] "In the middle of
dinner, she starts singing; she dances on her chair, pretends to
salute the world, makes the most terrible grimaces, rips the chick-
ens and partridges apart on their platters, and sticks her finger in
the sauces."[7] Sometimes she spent the night outdoors, when the

mood took her, running through the gardens all by herself. Mme de Maintenon, the duc de Saint-Simon, the whole court was shocked. But the extravagant behavior of the duchess did not cause their world to totter, did not throw the whole ceremonial of Versailles into question: it was, rather, the exception that proved the rule. Three quarters of a century later, Marie-Antoinette's insubordinate behavior, by contrast, seriously jeopardized that world.

Marie-Antoinette consumed life within the magic euphoria of immediate effects. That is why she was fond of charity and never tired of the spectacle of her own goodness. She might well have adopted the vicomte de Valmont's phrase, in *Dangerous Liaisons*: "I was stunned by the pleasure one feels in doing good." She built on this pleasure all her life. Individual incidents vary, but all are worthy of the comtesse de Ségur's novels. During a hunt at Fontainebleau, for example, a peasant was wounded by a stag. His wife fainted. Marie-Antoinette, still a mere dauphine, leapt out of her carriage and flew to the poor woman's aid. She gave her a whiff of perfume, offered her money, consoled her. This scene was reported by Mercy-Argenteau: "In the end, much moved, the archduchess shed a tear, and in that moment caused more than a hundred spectators around her to do likewise; they remained paralyzed by sudden emotion and admiration for such a unique and moving scene."[8] During the particularly hard winter of 1784, Marie-Antoinette provided her children with "a lesson in doing good" (in Mme Campan's words) by showing them the toys she would not buy them, instead using that money to distribute blankets and bread among children in need. The following year, the queen lodged and fed twelve poor families at Trianon. She founded the Society of Ladies of Maternal Charity, and so on.

Certain of her initiatives went sour — the adoption of the peasant boy Jacques, for instance, typical of the blindness of the rich as they stoop over the misery of the poor. It all began one day, when the queen's carriage nearly ran over a child. As Mme Campan reminisced:

> His grandmother sprang from the door of her cottage to grab him; but the queen, standing up in the carriage and opening her arms to the old peasant woman, cried that the child was hers, that fate had given him to her to comfort her, no doubt, until the moment she would be blessed with one of her own. "Does he have a mother?" she asked. "No, Madame, my daughter died last winter, leaving me with five grandchildren under my wing." "I'll take this one and look after the rest; do you give me your consent?" Her Majesty's arrival in her apartments at Versailles holding this little lout by the hand shocked her entire personnel; he screamed at the top of his lungs that he wanted his grandmother, his brother Louis, his sister Marianne; nothing could calm him down. He was carted off by the wife of a valet appointed to serve as his maid. The other children were sent to boarding school. Little Jacques, nicknamed Armand, returned to the queen two days later. A white suit, lace, a pink scarf with a silver fringe, and a hat decorated with feathers had replaced his woollen bonnet, his little red skirt, and clogs: the child was really very pretty. The queen was charmed.[9]

Jacques-Armand, apparently, much less so. Mme Campan recounted his ingratitude in a footnote: "The poor unfortunate was nearly twenty in 1792; the inflammatory talk of the people and fear of being considered one of the queen's favorites had made him the most bloodythirsty terrorist of Versailles. He was killed in the battle of Jemmapes."[10] It was indeed his sister Marianne whom he had wanted, as he'd cried out in those first few moments at Versailles! ...

Because she loved toying with appearances, Marie-Antoinette was most enthusiastic in another area where instantaneous transformation triumphs, where the success of an image flashes like lightning: fashion. *No Tomorrow* (1777), the title of Vivant Denon's libertine depiction of the fickle, intermittent nature of casual love, might also serve as the title for the enterprise of beauty pursued in the name of fashion. Marie-Antoinette had a profound affinity for fashion, an affinity profoundly scandalous in the eyes of her contemporaries. This heiress by divine right left every detail of her dress to the whim of the moment. In so doing, she admitted an element of instability, a craving for the new, into a world that strove to be atemporal. At court she promoted the taste for fashion which already governed certain aspects of Parisian life. The baronne d'Oberkirch, that tame provincial, was stupefied by the havoc fashion was wreaking on Parisian manners. "After the opera, we went to the Tuileries, which is the promenade in vogue. As Parisians do everything out of caprice, they have adopted one single path in the gardens and refuse to put a foot in any of the others. It is suffocating, one practically does battle there. The buttons on the men's clothes hook onto the lace on the ladies' capes, frills are torn by the hilts of swords, and sometimes whole trimmings remain dangling at the end of a scabbard."[11]

Fashion is, in its own way, a passion for the absolute, of which Marie-Antoinette was a fervent disciple. She, who grew up under her glorious ancestors' portraits, whose heavy baroque frames weighted down the rooms of Schönbrunn castle with gold, devoted herself unstintingly to the reign of the ephemeral. She consecrated as essential the gather of a flounce or the placing of a bouquet at the neckline of a fichu. Marie-Antoinette was both a follower of fashion and a trendsetter. Her physical type, her fair complexion, blonde hair, blue eyes, the porcelain fineness of her Saxon features, all answered exactly to the tastes of a new era, which banished brunettes and fawned over the quivering beauty and touching grace of blondes.

Good and beautiful: that's what Marie-Antoinette wanted to be and doubtless what she was. But that was not the media image that carried the day in a nation on the verge of revolution. A tragic contretemps, since, paradoxically, the marriage between princesses and fashion has since become their raison d'être. Nowadays princesses parade around in famous couturiers' latest designs. Newspapers and magazines celebrate queens as ambassadors of fashion. They must embody elegance — and charity. When they're not at fashion parades, they're busy doing good and may even, to this end, deploy treasures of inventiveness (thus we learn that "Princess Irene of the Netherlands and her three children Jaime, Margarita and Marie-Carolina de Bourbon-Parme have made a record, in Dutch, to help the poor families of Manila who would like to educate their children but don't have the money").... It is indeed unjust that Marie-Antoinette perished as a representative of the ancien régime, for, in fairness, she is the one who invented the *modern* princess, a heroine whose mass appeal needs no demonstration.

Rouge

Between 1770 and 1780, in their effort to create a stir, beautiful women continued to enlist the aid of artifice. In the fashion world, as we know, the natural is the height of art.[12] And the natural responds to variable norms. Faces, until then dotted with beauty spots (as fashionable for men as for women), become more uniform, but the heavy application of rouge continued undaunted. Equal effort must be made to imagine the eighteenth-century faces or churches. Today the stone columns of those churches are bare. At the time, church columns and arches were painted, their yellows, blues, and reds harmonizing with the luminous stained glass windows and the congregation's shimmering clothes. Mass was then the worldly outing par excellence, a gaily colored festivity. For many women it was their only chance to show them-selves. The passage of the centuries has brought about a decolora-tion, for people as for monuments. (This progressive effacement, this buffing of glaring color, is registered just as strongly in the evolution of the French language, which, becoming daily more insubstantial, drops the concrete meaning of a term in favor of its abstract sense.)

Censure by good taste, by the bourgeoisie, who preferred gray or beige to hot pink or orange, did not exist at that time: aristo-cratic pride went hand in hand with the idea of expenditure and a conspicuous presence. Like clothes, makeup declared confidence in the external signs of power. So the rouge of Versailles was worn redder than anywhere else: "Princesses wear it very bright and very strong in tone and they insist that women who are to be presented accentuate their rouge more than usual the day of their presentation...."[13] — thereby fixing the flush of vanity that such an honor could not fail to arouse! On other less official occasions, heavily plastered-on rouge spared one the duty of blushing. While it often compensated for a lack of modesty, it was even more precious as an antidote to the ravages of age. In a letter to her mother, Marie-Antoinette spoke of "the rouge that old ladies continue to wear here, sometimes even slightly more than young people. For the rest," she adds, "after forty-five, they wear less bright, less striking colors, looser, heavier dresses, their hair is less curled, and their hairdos less high."[14] Gérard de Nerval saw as a sign of the age's decrepitude the powder that, replacing wigs, gave everyone a white head toward the end of the eighteenth century. But if one thinks of the rouge that flourished on even the most crumpled cheeks, one may, conversely, see signs of that epoch's eternal youthfulness.

The "Bird's Nest"

Only twenty-one when she sent her mother this little chronicle on Versailles fashion, Marie-Antoinette did not fall in the hairdo-lowering category. She actually built hers up as high as possible, despite Mesdames' disapproval and her mother's remonstrations. She was reminded of the dignity of her role. She was told repeatedly that she should not get herself up like some actress or mistress. Marie-Antoinette did not deny her coquetry: "It is true that I am concerned with my appearance."[15] To reassure the empress, she offered to send "drawings of her different hairstyles" in one of her next letters (though she neglected to do so).

Hairdos in the mid-seventeen seventies reached staggering proportions. To achieve their chef d'oeuvres, hairdressers had to stand on a ladder. Women began traveling at knee height, carried on chairs. Certain doors become impractical. Caricatures of the time show hairdos catching fire, like sheaves of wheat, in candelabras hanging from the ceiling. But the dangers and drawbacks were immaterial: court ladies and elegant provincials had no choice. Surmounted by their "bird's nests," they hardly dared move. But height was not the only consideration, fantasy was also called into play. The hairdresser must not only have an architect's talent, he must also be a chronicler of events! Fashionable women had a choice between "the pouf with feeling," "bonnets at orchestra," "in an English park," "candid" coiffures, "Minervas," "Cleopatras," "Dianas," "the beautiful hen," "the globe of the world," "the barouche," and so on. They carried the world on their heads. And if they were bent on demonstrating their interest in current affairs, they could request "the inoculation" (after Louis XV's death from smallpox in 1774, the inoculation of closely related blue-blood princes hit the headlines of the gazettes) or "the Quesaco" (for the more cultured, who found this allusion to one of Beaumarchais's plays terribly chic). In the same register, note "the Iphigénie," a reference to the staging of Gluck's opera thanks to the queen's support, and, in a more political vein, "the insurgent," "the liberty," and "the Philadelphia," all evoking the American Revolution. More directly menacing for coiffed heads, some women wore "the bonnet of revolt," an erudite scaffolding of curls and ribbons inspired by an outbreak of famine in Paris after a hike in the price of bread. These baroque, artificial, provocative constructions evoke stylistic inventions of our own fin de siècle. They can only be seen as flirtations with catastrophe. "Cock's crest bonnets," for example, twisted hairstyles sculpted to form mountain peaks or cathedral spires were veritable announcements of their imminent collapse.

Why get yourself up like this if not to make the fall all the more glorious? The folly of the high hairdo was moving because it was an invitation to disaster: an admiral's wife wore the sea on her head, an endless interweaving of waves. The tiniest movement, the least disturbance of one of these waves, was sufficient to bring down the whole creation.

Crazy about this fashion, Marie-Antoinette, as queen, courted disaster. She did so as soon as she decided to entrust her hair to a fashionable hairdresser, thereby flouting the tradition of assigning to the queens of France a titled hairdresser who acquitted the honorific post in sober fashion and who alone had the right to touch the royal head. By calling on the services of a male hairdresser then in vogue, Marie-Antoinette offered up her head to the common touch. Worse, she encouraged the man to diversify his practices in the further exercise of his talent. Marie-Antoinette protected the sovereignty of the "creative artist," Léonard; in so doing, she perpetrated the double scandal of having a hairdresser who was not exclusively attached to the queen's service and of having a man occupy a function hitherto reserved for women. "At the time," wrote Mme de Genlis, "there were lady hairdressers for women; it would have been considered indecent to have one's hair done by a man. A year later, the hairdresser Larseneur of Versailles was all the rage for young women's debuts.... Soon male hairdressers were established in Paris; *finally Léonard arrived*, and all the lady hairdressers fell into disrepute and obscurity."[16]

Léonard's success ended with the Revolution (success both as a hairdresser and as the queen's faithful servant, for his assistance to the queen, during the flight to Varennes was a disaster: "It was to master Léonard, most devoted but not terribly bright, that the queen entrusted her diamonds and the task of assisting Choiseul in the flight to Varennes; of course everything went haywire."[17]) The ever higher hairdos collapsed with the expression "to have oneself clipped" (that is, to be sent to the guillotine). Michelet assures us that "the most rabid royalists were perhaps neither nobles, nor priests, but wigmakers."[18] After the Terror, they could not resurrect the old spirit of construction. With the abundant crop of hair, cut wigs now fetched low prices.

The bond between wigmakers and the nobility was reciprocal. While the wigmakers lost their clientele during the Revolution, the aristocracy, deprived of their services, dragged out their days in the courtyards of the prisons of Saint-Pélagie and the Abbey, their hair disheveled, unpowdered, and unwashed.

Hair That Incites Hatred

According to Fleischmann, "The first attacks against the queen, which were rather moderate, belonging more to the spoken complaint than to the pamphlet, began with the fad for high hairdos that held sway around 1775."[19] These fairy-floss constructions excited public derision. Later, by 1789, the tone had shifted from laughter to reprobation. Exciting ridicule, the high hairstyle provoked reactions of sexual and political disgust. In its classifieds, *Le*

Petit Journal listed these objects for sale: "The complete toiletry of the duchesse de Duras, consisting of all known accessories, individually, false teeth, false chignons, false toupees, false curls, and a false MOUND OF VENUS, invented by the queen's hairdresser, former director of Monsieur's theater."[20] The press mingled excitement and revulsion. It also warned against the seductive assets of Marie-Antoinette, who would stop at nothing to strengthen the royalist party. Suckers fall for her long hair; the pamphlets denounce "lovers of her red mane." Marie-Antoinette's red "mane" (sometimes associated with the red hair of Judas) is deployed in the revolutionaries' imagination like a bloody standard.

Hair That Pledges Tenderness

Maria Theresa sent her daughter locks of her hair. "They are my pride and joy," Marie-Antoinette responded, adding that she has had them mounted in a ring and a heart-shaped pendant. Touched, Maria Theresa replied, "Madame, my dear daughter, I am most relieved that my old gray hair wanted to give you so much pleasure...."[21] The energy of Maria Theresa's language is such that her errors and idiosyncracies in French always say what she means. She remains present even when something — in language or in nature — prevents her from writing: "Forgive the blots and corrections in this one; I had three goes at writing, and the wind blew them away twice. You know what winds reign in my room."[22] Certain passages in the letters of Maria Theresa evoke Mme de Sévigné. Maternal passion, barely distinguishable from the empress's political passion, is similarly vital and possessive. Both women try, through their letters, to maintain their hold, to control in an authoritarian manner the fecund bodies of their daughters: Mme de Grignan lets herself get pregnant too often for her mother's liking; Marie-Antoinette, not often enough.

The Taste for Feathers

The use of feathers in high hairstyles particularly excited derision, as though the mobile plumes symbolized all too clearly the guilty flightiness of these bird-brained women.

The rumors and pamphlets that attacked the queen's interest in her appearance thereby attacked her for being excessively female, that is, vicious. The amount of time and money she spent worshiping at the altar of fashion reeked of the sins of the flesh: the craze for finery was merely the most obvious manifestation of more secret crazes, more perverse debauchery — betraying these, if not actually inspiring them. Wasn't the fashion for feather hairstyles directly responsible for a certain sexual quirk, which crops up several times in the pornographic press of the day? In *The Almanach of Honest Women for the Year 1790*, a taste for feathers is attributed to a M. Peixotte (or Pexioto): "The little Jew undressed his mistress, stuck peacock feathers up her bum, and got her to walk around the room on all fours; then he put his hands under her rump and cried: 'Oh! What a beautiful bird!' He himself was subject to the same metamorphosis and after a few moments' ecstasy, he finished by taking the place of the feathers." *The Libertine Catechism* offers the same quirk, here attributed to a priest rather than a Jew (both represent perverse characters in revolutionary propaganda): "Then he takes a lovely peacock's tail feather out of his pocket and unbuttons his trousers; he lies on my bed with his bum in the air and asks me to place the end of the feather in his arse, and I do; then to caress his bum, saying the words: 'Ah! What a beautiful peacock!'"[23]

These vicious pavans are one extreme of the simple charge of sacrificing too much to fashion. The taste for adornment is never far from the debauchery of the brothel. It is only a skip and a jump from coquette queen to prostitute queen. "The most elegant whore in Paris could not be more tarted up than the queen," in the words of the anonymous author of *Historical Essays on the Life of Marie-Antoinette of Austria, Queen of France.*

The Queen's Dresses

At the staging of her beauty, it was the queen who commanded. Every morning she consulted the ledger of frivolity. The first decision of Marie-Antoinette's day was the choice of her outfits. The catalog of samples from her wardrobe was brought to her as soon as she awoke, immediately after her cup of coffee. She would choose from among the several patterns pinned to paper. The dresses she wore were the object of amorous attention on her part. She sometimes happened to launch a style, such as the "queen's shirt" (*chemise à la reine*) (a wide dress with flounces, attached sleeves, décolleté, the neck decorated with a strawberry), in vogue in 1780. But most of the dresses she wore were the creation of Mlle Bertin, her favorite couturier. Marie-Antoinette's recognition of Mlle Bertin's talents went even as far as authorizing her to enter the queen's apartments. Protocol on this point had hitherto been so strict that, when a doctor from the court of Vienna came to visit Versailles, Marie-Antoinette had to intervene to allow him to enter her room. Mlle Bertin, on the other hand, had no trouble threading her way through the court. She enjoyed more privileges than the high and mighty. (In this as well, Marie-Antoinette showed herself to be thoroughly modern, giving the art of fashion the place it enjoys today.)

Critics of the queen's costly coquetry targeted her exalted purveyor. Labelled the "female minister," Rose Bertin was, in the eyes of the public, the incarnation of arbitrary royal preferences — and the financial gains to be made from them. The couturier also symbolized the decadence that Marie-Antoinette was alleged to have introduced into French life and at court. In opposition to the virile ideal essential to the imaginary of the Revolution, Marie-

Antoinette represented a principle of *effeminacy*: "As her Minister for Trinkets, the queen has taken on la Bertin, Fashion Merchant.... Another female minister is the dancer Guimard, of the Paris Opera, Minister for Muslin and Costumes...."[24] (A century later, Ludwig II of Bavaria rose to the level of pamphlet exaggeration. From his Bavarian Trianon, he sent the court hairdresser Hoppe to Munich to form a new ministerial cabinet ... No one believed in the Devil any more in the nineteenth century — charges of mental illness were levelled instead; psychiatrists have replaced judges. Marie-Antoinette went before a tribunal which declared her guilty and condemned her to the guillotine. Ludwig II was deposed on the strength of a medical report which concluded that "His Majesty is no longer fit to exercise government and this incapacity will last not only more than a year but for the rest of his life." His Majesty was condemned to suicide.)

Marie-Antoinette, the "Trinket Queen," perverted the seriousness of affairs of state. Under her reign, the most grave problems were treated with more nonchalance than a point of fashion. Marie-Antoinette's occult power appeared all the more pernicious symbolizing as it did the power of feminine weakness. The pamphlets denounced a chain of influences: a weak king is manipulated by his wife, who is herself under the thumb of a couturier. The king's will goes no further than the circumference of the queen's frocks.

Mme Roland, whose philosophical head refused to sacrifice to fashion's feathers, was indignant to find, on venturing into the world of the salons, that "effeminate men proclaim their admiration for slender verses, aimless talents."[25] An enemy of the queen, she knew how to subtly insinuate the queen's sly presence. She recounts a conversation between Louis XVI and Pétion, the mayor of Paris, in the following terms: "The faint rustling of silk behind the curtain persuaded Pétion that the queen was present without being visible, and the caresses of the king convinced him of his falseness: he remained firm and honest without yielding to the prince, who was trying to corrupt him...."[26]

We find a similar scene involving Marie-Antoinette's clandestine eavesdropping in the words of another woman, this time in praise of the queen's marvelous discretion. Mme de Genlis had come with the court to the château de Marly. She was in the habit of playing music in her room before bed:

> One night, between eleven o'clock and midnight, while I was playing the harp as I usually do, sight-reading a sonata, to my great surprise M. d'Avaray entered the room and whispered that the queen was in Mme de Valbelle's room, where she had come in order to hear me playing the harp. I immediately began playing the pieces and songs I knew best, which went on for an hour and a half without interruption, as I was waiting for a movement in the next room to tell me the queen was getting up to go; but there was absolute silence. In the end, genuinely exhausted, I stopped. Immediately, there were several bursts of vigorous applause and M. d'Avaray came to thank me for the queen, and he said wonderful things on her behalf. She repeated these to me the next day when I went to pay court.[27]

This anecdote, formally analogous to the one recounted by Mme Roland, works similarly to define a power exercised in the shadows, behind a partition, a curtain, a screen — an indeterminate but omniscient power, traditionally that of women. This is precisely what Mme Roland repudiated, influenced as she was by Rousseau, who abhorred the power of women and of the dark in equal measure. The honesty, frankness, and virility of a republican government was to stand in opposition to royalty, corrupted as it was at its (dark) source by the invisible omnipresence of the queen. The spineless drip of a king was the slave of the coquette queen. The entire realm was pervaded by weakness, falseness, the effeminate. When all is said and done, as Louise Robert wrote in 1791, the worst thing about kings is queens. These "crowned sirens" overstep their authority, from the conjugal bed to the state. From deep within their boudoirs, they rule over "the marching of armies, the fate of colonies." So, the author concludes, "Peoples who have not yet grown tired of kings should at least insist that they be atheists, bastards, and eunuchs."[28]

The queen whose splendor was bleeding the people dry — a theme overworked to the point of insinuating vampirism — became a favorite motif of the scandal sheets. Beaumarchais's continued employment as prosecutor of the gutter press was significant. First hired by Louis XV to destroy the lampoons directed against Mme du Barry, Beaumarchais was taken on by the king's successor to attack lampoonists hostile to Marie-Antoinette. Du Barry, whose life roused Théveneau de Morande's ire in his celebrated *Anecdotes Concerning the comtesse du Barry*, exemplified the confusion between court and brothel. Indeed, she went directly from Jean du Barry, a cunning and seductive pimp ("She's his milking cow," one police report baldly states), to the bed of the king. Du Barry's coquetry is legendary: her two greatest pleasures, Théveneau wrote, were "doing nothing and being constantly engaged in dressing up."[29] All part of her profession.

The snickering over Marie-Antoinette's coquetry should be understood in the context of the aftermath of criticism of du Barry's costly ostentation: the queen inherited the favorite's renown; she was assigned both roles. Exceptional in the history of France, Marie-Antoinette was both queen and favorite simultaneously — Louis XVI having acquired the bourgeois taste of being faithful to one's wife. This situation, far from serving Marie-Antoinette's image, contributed to the public's attributing every vice to her. As sovereign, she was above the law. As favorite, she ruled over the king and subjugated the court to her pleasure. Marie-Antoinette combined the faults of the first role (arrogance, the arbitrariness of absolute sovereignty) with those of the second (duplicity, obsession with appearances). In the eyes of the public, her ruinous coquetry perpetuated the ostentation of du Barry, who, it was said, was having a dress of gold made for her while Louis XV lay dying. The nasty epigram aimed at Mme du Barry — "France what is your destiny? / To be crushed by a Female / Your salvation came from a Virgin [Joan of Arc] / You will perish under the Prostitute" — seemed even truer under the reign of Marie-Antoinette.

Next to the catalog of the queen's dresses, brought to her first thing every morning, one could place the accusing *Le Livre rouge* (printed in April 1790), which offers, along with proof of the greed of those in favor, proof of her spendthrift vanity. The simplistic notion of a country being ruined by one woman's expenditure is obviously pure fantasy. The height of a hairstyle, gold dresses, and shoes with diamond buckles did not cause a state to crumble. On the stage of history, however dolled up and fascinating they may be, queens and favorites are ever only extras.

Immanent Justice

Biographers, historians, and novelists are particularly keen to point out, as so much proof of the vanity of an immoral life and its ineluctable punishment, the marks of decrepitude in hardened libertines. That is why they never get tired of imagining Casanova's old age (he himself was silent about the third act of his life). It is precisely this fall into the common lot that excites posterity's interest: *even he* ends up getting old. This event, which isn't one, is banal, pitiful. The famous libertine, the glamorous playboy, must admit defeat, admit that he is barred from the

exceptional destiny he had dared to choose. A moralizing discourse, more or less explicit, comments on the fornicator's defeat: "Heavens! Look what the years have done to him. He is ugly,
broken, unrecognizable. He totters about the empty rooms of a
castle, somewhere on the northern plains. The servants shun his
caresses. The cooks mock his accent. So this is the great Casanova,
this grotesque old man!" This retrospective slaughter is all the
more pleasurable because old age, far from being gradual, almost
imperceptible, appears to occur overnight, striking like the Last
Judgment or the intervention of the Commander at the end of
Don Juan.

Marie-Antoinette also delighted her enemies with the spectacle of losing her looks. The woman they liked to represent as a
libertine using and abusing her charms suddenly became an old
woman. And, as with Casanova, they never ceased comparing her
premature physical ruin with her stunning past beauty. Old age
for the debauched is not access to a superior dignity. These people
have learned nothing, understood nothing. It is useless hoping
that they will convert.

Just after the dauphin's death in 1789, Marie-Antoinette's hair
turned white. The episode is well known. No account of it fails to
mention the sudden transformation of the young woman. Fleischmann depicts her "thin face with its halo of hair turned white
from captivity." Gérard Walter describes her "physical collapse"
with conviction: "In the very rare official ceremonies where she is
still obliged to appear, excessively made up, and thanks to her
hairdresser and her dressmaker, the queen succeeds in hiding her
decrepitude, but close up the ravages her body is in the process of
suffering are alarmingly visible. She cannot stop losing weight.
Her breasts sag. Her inflamed face is covered with pimples. Her
eyes have become dull and sunken. Saliva continually wets the
corners of her mouth."[30] In this quasi-medical tone, which scarcely

obscures acute revulsion, an ideology of truth is enunciated: the sudden laying bare of a woman's abominable nature, illusorily veiled by the glamour of appearances and the attractions of youth. Aged libertines are not only punished; in the end, according to the denouement of Laclos's *Dangerous Liaisons,* they wear their souls on their faces.

That Marie-Antoinette's soul might have nothing in common with a libertine's had no bearing on such representations of decrepitude. To underscore the disparity between her behavior and, say, Mme de Merteuil's intellectual and sexual audacity, let us recall that Marie-Antoinette's most wildly "libertine" exploits included such extravagances as wanting to see the sun rise (which immediately prompted a pamphlet) or continuing to go for donkey rides, despite her mother's haranguing her not to. And in Marie-Antoinette's antipathy toward Mme du Barry, one can detect a purely emotional reaction, primarily betraying her sense of rank and birth and her absolute contempt for a "common whore" — but also her sense of virtue. Warned that she would meet Mme du Barry the following day, Marie-Antoinette was deeply disturbed. "I was anxious about the indecisiveness I noticed the day before. I went to Mme the Dauphine's," Mercy-Argenteau reported. "She was just back from mass. 'I prayed hard,' she told me. 'I said, "Lord, if you want me to speak, make me speak; I will do whatever you deign to inspire me!"'"[31] The Lord inspired her to say "The weather is bad, one can't go for walks during the day" — but her utterance was so lacking in conviction that it went unnoticed. A few days later, she would be divinely inspired to say to Mme du Barry that "There are a lot of people at Versailles today," an observation that spread through the courtiers like a powder trail. (At court, it was not the content of a sentence that mattered, but the fact that the king or queen, in pronouncing it, bestowed on the happy recipient the grace of their favor. Naturally, it was forbidden to address the former first. The extreme violation of this interdiction was found in the situation of a king appearing before a tribunal and being there only to *answer* the questions of his accusers. This reversal of all the rules of speech contributed to the sincere bewilderment of Louis XVI, who confided to his valet, after a hearing during his trial: "I was far from being able to think about all the questions they put to me.") Before the spectacle of Louis XV's passion for Mme du Barry, the woman Marie-Antoinette called "that creature," she must have felt curiosity, disgust, and perhaps fear, face to face with an unknown world ruled entirely by sensuality.

The immanent justice that caught up with libertines was scarcely appropriate for Marie-Antoinette, except in the register of the blithely improbable, wherein pamphlet writing is located. "No one could differ as much as she from the reputation her enemies have tried to pin on her," Mme de Staël remarked. "One did not even try to find the slightest grain of truth in the lie, one was so aware of that envy which is more than happy to satisfy slanderers' expectations."[32]

A Less Familiar Ending

What if, sensing that justice for her would not stop at the loss of her fair complexion, Marie-Antoinette had had the idea of getting away, of entrusting to a double (since the Diamond Necklace Affair had revealed to her that it was her fate to give rise to doubles) the task of carrying on?

Definitively discouraged in her role as queen by the death of her son, Marie-Antoinette decides to tackle other roles. She leaves Versailles at dawn, wrapped in a large coat. She secretly signs up with a traveling Italian theater group and faces a real audience for the first time a few nights later. In her private theater at Trianon she has only performed before the royal family and a few servants who don't count. But now she must conquer a crowd of strangers. Little by little she learns how.

Her past slips away from her. She speaks and dreams in Italian. One autumn day, on tour in a small spa town where the river has already frozen, she hears that the queen of France has been guillotined. While donning her harlequin costume, she thinks what a lucky break she has had and leaps with wild joy onto the stage.

Simplicité Oblige

In prison, Louis XVI and Marie-Antoinette's daughter, Marie Thérèse Charlotte, then fifteen years old, was interrogated in the presence of the painter Jacques-Louis David. When asked how her father and mother were dressed on the flight to Varennes, she replied, "Quite simply." Indeed, in the course of that trip, the royal family made enormous efforts at simplicity, more symbolic than practical, for they could not bear to travel in anything other than a huge berlin, which was comfortable but not very fast. The king "quite simply" assumed the name Durand. He played first valet to Mme de Tourzel (governess to the royal family's children), who was traveling under the pseudonym baronne de Korff. The queen was content to be Mme Rochet, but the public, unable to allow her a common name, caricatured her as a panther on her return from Varennes, calling her "Her Excellency the baronne de Korff." She systematically focused the people's hatred through her haughtiness, her imperious deportment (captured in a well-known David drawing). It was as though, shorn of her flowers, dresses, and jewels, thin, discolored, and hairless, she identified herself with the rigidity of a conviction. The latter triumphed, inflexible, in the harsh lines of her profile.

Endless attempts were made to bring the proud Antoinette down. Prison was thought to be the ideal place to add to her troubles.

There, the queen literally "came undone." Louis XVI's valet told how the royal family had been given linen marked with crowned letters when they were locked up in the Temple; municipal officers then forced the princesses to remove the embroidered crowns. Marie-Antoinette, who had, according to Nerval, been "embroidered in all kinds of stitches," had to unpick the last vestiges of her splendor herself.

The revolutionaries relentlessly targeted Marie-Antoinette's desire to seduce. They could not punish her enough. The contemporary critic Pierre Saint-Amand deftly followed the process of "gradual disfigurement" the queen was made to suffer: "What an irony ... that the person who had brought her own seamstress to Versailles should now spend her time mending. Later, they took away Marie-Antoinette's scissors; she is described sewing her undergarments and breaking the thread with her teeth. The queen maintained her love of fabrics right up to the end, almost as if her narcissism had been transferred to the cloth as last vestige of self adoration." After she was beheaded, Saint-Amand went on, "the remains of Marie-Antoinette's clothes were sent to a hospital, to be worn by women who were never to know the identity of the original owner."[33] They absolutely hounded the phantoms of beauty the queen left behind her.

Marie-Antoinette's shoe.

Lavcugle Mal Conduit

Under Marie-Antoinette's reign, the devil himself is feminine, hideously feminine....

CHAPTER FOUR

The Female Monster

How can I accomplish this great work? O Shrew,
inspire me ... Ah! your genius speaks to me, I feel it in
the raptures that inflame me and bring me back to life.
— *Historical Essays on the Life of Marie-Antoinette*

Barnave's Bust

Barnave's bust is on display in the Carnavalet Museum in Paris.
The Girondin deputy is represented as a young man, full of the
fiery energy of his revolutionary zeal. His gaping shirt reveals a
chest from which the breath of an orator sprang. The bust is an emblem of the public man, modeled on the great men of antiquity.

In another room, much less visible, a fragment of embroidered
silk is on display, from one of Marie-Antoinette's dresses, pre-
served by Barnave and found on him at his death. How can we
reconcile this amorous fetish with the preceding bust? Torn apart
by his passion, Barnave himself found it impossible.

Insatiable Marie-Antoinette

Just as others carry a love letter to the grave, Barnave climbed the
scaffold with a souvenir in his pocket: that piece of the queen's
dress, proof of his guilty love, a shred of the world he had fought

to destroy. In the following century, Edmond and Jules de Goncourt spent their lives psychologically clinging to a piece of the queen's dress. They lived, dreamed, and wrote in the wake of her train. Steeped in reactionary nostalgia and contempt for the bourgeois mentality of their contemporaries, they worshiped the image of the queen. But Barnave's love affair was born of an actual meeting with the queen, in the dramatic circumstances of the fugitives' return to Paris after their arrest at Varennes. According to Walter, "Marie-Antoinette tried to hold a conversation with Barnave, who remained silent or answered in monosyllables. She did not insist, savoring her conquest. Indeed, when the royal family set out, Barnave was no longer sulking. He settled down once again beside the queen and, this time, would not change places all the way to Paris. The moment the carriage stopped in front of the castle, Marie-Antoinette said playfully to him: 'I must admit I did not think we would spend thirteen hours together.'"[1] In Walter's narrative, Marie-Antoinette continues to play the seductress, despite her already advanced physical decay — according to the author. Fortified by the demon that inspired her, she concluded this terrible journey, which made prisoners of her family, with a gaiety more appropriate to coming home from a day in the country. Barnave let himself be seduced.

Against all his revolutionary convictions and simple common sense, Barnave took on the risk of loving. For the Goncourt brothers, on the contrary, devotion to the "Century of Woman" and the woman who reigned supreme over it served to avoid encountering real women. The Goncourts loved growing up together so much that they could not resist the desire to grow old together. In the tranquillity of celibacy they re-created the book of the queen's dresses, with the patience of children cutting out and dressing up paper dolls. These "coquettish relics" (their own term) helped them to forget the fetid reality of sex. In other words, the reconstructive and phantasmic minutiae of their writings in no way touched on the nudity of the queen, "an honest woman ... a pure woman."[2] Their biography of Marie-Antoinette proceeded from an obsession with purity — the exact opposite of the nasty vein feeding the literature of the pamphlets. For the Goncourts, common women represented vice. "There were even women whom the revolution made unnatural to their own sex. Modesty already had a very slim hold on the women who, in 1791, filled the hall at Châtelet for a rape case. It was defunct in those unhappy women whose hands had to be tied later during their trial to stop them from tucking up their skirts; and defunct in those girls, condemned for murder, who went to the guillotine singing dirty songs!"[3] According to an author's royalist or revolutionary persuasion, the prize for feminine chastity passed from one camp to the other — as though proof of the superiority of a political regime depended on the degree of women's virtue.

The same misogyny ends in two antithetical attitudes to the persona of Marie-Antoinette. She was Queen of Vice for the lampoonists of the eighteenth century. She crudely manifests the fundamental truth expressed plainly in the first article of the *Libertine Catechism*: "*Question*: Do all women have a definite tendency to become prostitutes? *Answer*: All of them are or want to be...." Conversely, she was the Queen of Virtue for the nineteenth century apologists, especially the Goncourts. She reinforced, by contrast, their disgust for real women. (To cure himself of his desire for women, Jules de Goncourt refused for a long time to treat a venereal disease he had caught from a prostitute.)

The love of fashion and detail at work when the Goncourts described the apparel of the past century, such as the dress decorated "with a trimming made of the feathers of four thousand jays," must have been useful to them in screening out the whole matter of sex from their lives — and that may be the use fashion had for Marie-Antoinette herself. However, in the lampoons, satires, and songs directed against the queen, love of fashion was just one sign among many of her vicious nature, her coquetry the visible manifestation of a hidden imbalance: spending big was the symptom of a maniacal greed. The endless debts of the queen's house pointed to depravities for which the services of a couturier were not enough for Marie-Antoinette.

As hatred of her grew, vain Marie-Antoinette, the feather-brained trinket queen, decked out like her gardens, became perverse Marie-Antoinette, dissolute queen of the burning womb. Her excesses reduced her to the subhuman (she was worse than an animal) or catapulted her far beyond humanity (she was a witch, a scourge, a vampire, the wicked queen of fairy tales). Her vices threatened not only the health of France's citizens and the nation's financial equilibrium, but the equilibrium of the world.

Marie-Antoinette was the harbinger of scandal. This foreign woman introduced into the court of France the dissolution and brutality of German morals. Despite the purification rites that marked her passage across the border, the taint was irremediable, the seed of evil too strong: the pamphlets that accuse Marie-Antoinette of outrageous licentiousness never fail to recall that she practiced vice in the German manner. The vigor of her temperament was the index of her foreign origins. *The Austrian Woman on the Rampage, or The Royal Orgy* (1789) (included in this volume) insists on the fact that only a foreign woman could behave so badly. Under the lampoonists' pens, the sacred ceremony of Reims became a farce, degrading to the dignity of Louis XVI and of France. Who was responsible? The queen, of course. And this fallen woman dared to boast about it: "I drank a fair bit — that is, like a good, loyal German. Warmed up by the liqueurs, I ran into the copse with my hair flying, looking rather like a bacchante; everyone followed my example."[4]

Bad Example personified, the queen never ceased to offer evidence of denaturation. Incapable of the slightest feeling of modesty, she was used to yielding to the ardor of her senses — in the middle of a coronation if necessary. Marie-Antoinette couldn't resist the incitement of a copse. In public or with her intimate friends, day or night, completely at the mercy of her "uterine furors," no flower bed was safe from her. She was the Attila of French gardens. "She ran through the groves of trees like a mad woman or rather, like a bacchante; everyone did likewise; and, at a certain sign, her friends blew out the candles. They wandered about looking for mischief. One adventurer grabbed the royal vagabond, and she often had no idea who the reckless soul was to whom she gave herself."[5] In these "realistic" scenes, the queen cannot be distinguished from the lowest prostitute; she blends in with the horde of "female fuckers, leg shakers, pavement beaters, nightwalkers, and hustlers of no fixed abode, jerking cocks off in public squares and crossroads."[6] However, and this is where the imagination falters, she remains *The Queen*. What very poor women do out of necessity, she gives herself over to out of vice.

In the pamphlets, Marie-Antoinette's erotic style was crude: "I have always loved rough and tumble affairs," she proclaimed frankly. "At the very sight of a good-looking man or a beautiful woman, my eyes would become inflamed, my face would change, you could see sexual pleasure written all over it. I could hardly conceal the violence of my desire and none of the objects of my lust ever escaped my tender loving care...."[7] Hatred, like sexual fantasy (and in Marie-Antoinette's case the two were inextricably linked), can happily accommodate contradictions. The same people who attacked the queen for her sly nature, her "effeminate" influence, her rococo taste, and her exaggerated aestheticism (or suprematism before the term existed: her white marble dairy built at Trianon concretely executed Malevitch's *White Square on White*. The queen loved white — she could have used Malevitch's phrase, "I have penetrated white," to describe herself), considered her a downright bawd. This coquette who brought France to its knees with fancy clothes, extravagant hairstyles, and a passion for jewels was also, equally, a dumb guttersnipe, drunk with fucking and blood, ready to violate whomever or whatever was in her grasp. She imported the consummate art of hypocrisy to Versailles, seconded in this by the abbé Vermond, her faithful private advisor and the voice of her conscience; at the same time, she imported the morals of a foreign army into a conquered country. It is indeed enough to make one quake in one's boots!

The murky legend of Marie-Antoinette would have her deflowered by a German soldier or, better still, by her brother, Joseph II: "The introduction of the *imperial priapus* into the *Austrian canal* led to the accumulation there, so to speak, of the passion of incest, the foulest pleasures, hatred of the French, aversion to the duties of wife and mother; in a word, everything that reduces humanity to the level of wild beasts."[8] While the deflowering of Marie-Antoinette by her brother is a fantasy, it is nonetheless undeniable that, had Joseph II not persuaded Louis XVI to remedy the phimosis that made him impotent, Marie-Antoinette would never have become a mother. The introduction of the "royal priapus" into the "Austrian canal" is indeed the result of an incestuous mediation. And when Joseph II caught up with his sister again after seven years' separation, he declared his pleasure to her in no uncertain terms: "He added that, were she not his sister and were he able to be joined with her, he would not think twice about remarrying in order to provide himself with such a charming companion...."[9]

The obscene engravings and pornographic pamphlets of the eighteenth century run the gamut of possibilities in their list of the queen's depravities. Austrian — that is, incestuous, alcoholic, bawdy, and bestial — she animated an infernally lubricious saga. She was the fabulous star of an imagery of evil all the more convincing for associating the blunders of the political regime with the eternal vices of Woman (here biblical teachings chimed in with the critical analyses of the Enlightenment). Through Marie-Antoinette, the pamphlets denounced the morals of the women at court. Under the influence of a prostitute queen, the court became a brothel. This highly selective space, allegedly gathering within it the flower of a realm, was little more than a bordello. The pamphlets can be read as the perfect expression of a reversal of values. They are the antiphrasis of the world of excellence described by Mme de La Fayette in her novel *The Princesse de Clèves* (1678), whose story unfolds under the reign of Henry II. "No court has ever brought together so many beautiful women and wonderfully handsome men; it seemed as if nature had bestowed her finest gifts on fair princesses and noble princes alike.... Those I shall name here were, in their different ways, the ornament and wonder of their age."[10] Conversely, the men and particularly the women the pamphlets name were the shame of theirs.

One may read, apropos the duchesse de Grammont, Choiseul's sister (and said to be linked to him by incest): "She was a woman of the court in all senses of the term, that is, determined, impudent, wild, and considering morals to be merely for the people."[11] What was true of Louis XV's court was even more true of Louis XVI's, thanks to his wife's charming nature. *A Red Heel's Wallet* sketches several portraits of women in Marie-Antoinette's court, all equally unworthy of a place in a precious novel. "See how [the duchesse de Châtillon] has her eyes riveted on the flies of all the young lords.... It costs her 4,000 francs a year for the pleasures of the cot. The Marquise de Fleury ... since her retirement, they say she has fallen very much in love with an actress called Raucourt."[12]

Another more virulent pamphlet denounced the women of Versailles as so many "whores and tribades, gamblers and frauds, generally the worst company in Europe."[13] According to the principle of inversion which associates greatness of rank with baseness of instinct, the royal princesses cop the worst: the king's sister-in-law, the comtesse de Provence "loves wine, men, women, gardens, furniture, and money, and to pursue these various tastes, whatever the cost, whether the king curses, her husband sulks, or the minister refuses, or there is a revolution, or the Estates General introduces reform; she couldn't give a damn. She wants pleasure, and pleasure she shall have."[14]

The scandal sheets ran riot representing feminine pleasure triumphant (which was intolerable to masculine pride). The tribades of Versailles, with the Austrian "arch tigress" at the helm, gave no quarter. The voracity of their desire drove traditional sex roles from the field. In their presence, the most innocent encounter turned into an orgy. Where order and decency reigned before they arrived, they mounted a spectacle — demoralizing for the people, both in terms of men's virility and women's virtue — of gender confusion and licence in all its forms. Of course, the orgiastic, tyrannical queen led the dance. In her insatiability, she forgot everything, even her prejudices about birth: "Nobility, clergy, third estate — any man has a right to her favors; the most handsome and robust are the most welcome: guards, lackeys, actors. Height of opprobrium! Oh, indelible shame!"[15] She mixed up all the estates, which is not the same thing as reinstating them in all their dignity.

The queen's versatility did not spring from capriciousness alone. It answered a need: Marie-Antoinette had to change partners incessantly, since no one could keep up with her for long. She exhausted them one by one: "This galant intercourse lasted until I was sick of the sameness, feigned indifference, and decided to provide the exhausted Fersen with some successor."[16] Every male reader of the salient facts about the ghoul of Versailles could identify with the "exhausted Fersen." It was a delicious terror, a rewriting of the worn-out Don Juan fable, in which the object seduced and abandoned is always a woman. Marie-Antoinette, alone representing the Hydra of the ancien régime, was only a coherent myth, an obsessive image, because she incarnated a more obscure fear: the fear of castration. The tiny ringlets of her fair down, her silly flocks of sheep, and her white marble dairy are only there, disarmingly innocent, all the better to hurl her victim into the death machine between her legs. The queen's power, having been exercised against the king, emasculated all the able-bodied men of her realm. The time had passed for jokes, for the complicit, ribald wink. One of Antoinette's caprices would suffice, just one of her lubricious whims, and myriad bacchantes, the infernal legion of the women of the court, would swoop down on Gallic virility like a cloud of locusts.

Now it was up to other women, the common women, who were the opposite of the race of court women, to go and get the queen at Versailles. (If, on this occasion, under the combined effects of fatigue, hunger, and alcohol, certain of them conduct themselves like bacchantes, this does not diminish their virtuous role.) The royal family's trip from Versailles to Paris, on October 6, 1789, marked by insults and threats, was the opposite of a triumphant royal entry. It was a journey of expiation, measured exactly according to Marie-Antoinette's "crimes": "And if all the cocks that have been in my cunt were put end to end, they would stretch all the way from Paris to Versailles," the queen declares in *The Patriotic Bordello*.[17] In the logic of this sexual madness, Marie-Antoinette ought to have entered Paris preceded, like the infamous Roman emperor Heliogabalus, by a gigantic phallus.

The "Hopeless Potentate"

The debauchery of Louis XVI's wife could not be taken lightly, for it trampled underfoot the sacred modesty of women and their pro-creative vocation; and, in making a cuckold of the king, it under-mined the dignity of all men in the realm.

Marie-Antoinette's sexual superpowers have as their corollary the hopelessness of the king. The licentious wife of an impotent spouse was the stuff of farce, causing laughter when it affected mere commoners. But it was not so funny when it concerned the sovereign couple, because then it was a sign that something was rotten in the state of France. The vision of Marie-Antoinette, weary from pleasure, beside her august and impotent husband, was intolerable, as much from the royalist as from the revolution-ary point of view. Louis XVI's hopeless sex life for the first seven years of his marriage provided endless grist for the pamphleteers' mill. One pamphlet mocked "a young and frisky Queen / Whose most August Spouse was a bad fuck,"[18] while *The Uterine Furors of Marie-Antoinette, Wife of Louis XVI* observed that "The Sire was so limp / that Toinon's eyes, and all the arts of the right hand / could do nothing…"

In her infidelities, the queen's methods were not overly subtle. *The Austrian Woman on the Rampage* showed her being taken by the comte d'Artois, the king's brother, on the very back of Louis XVI as he sleeps, tuckered out by all his tinkering with locks. But if the king could not see, he could drink. The impotent cuckold king was also, in the logic of the populist fable, a drunk. A letter from the queen to her lover, Cardinal Rohan, told of the sad state of affairs prevailing under the gold wainscoting of Versailles: "Then she spoke of the unpleasant night she had spent with the king. All the expressions she used were of contempt and disgust. She made particular allusion to the vice of drink.…"

The king needed not even be drunk or dead tired to attend the orgies that made a mockery of him. In *Capuchins in Motion*, Louis XVI was simply "sprawled in his armchair in the middle of the room." Holding hands, the queen, Polignac, and a few priests formed a debauched ring around him, singing some moronic song. That "big ninny of a husband," "the idiot king," "the royal cuckold," "the null potentate" should never have married the arch bitch of Austria, that slut capable of laying waste to the gallant tradition of the kings of France. The king's mistresses, by contrast — now there's a fine subject for reverie! The French love to remember the amorous tyranny of Louis XIV, who exiled any courtier bold enough to glance at a woman the king desired; or Louis XV's Parc-aux-Cerfs (Stag Park), that sumptuous harem where young girls were brought to him to be deflowered, a paradise of royal fornication built with the enthusiastic collaboration of the greatest libertines of the age! But what did Louis XVI contribute to kingly depravity? Nothing, absolutely nothing. Not one sin of the flesh, not a single temptation to confess. This was the regime of the "royal zero," as Léon Bloy spitefully called him, adding, "Louis XVI did not have a mistress, and that is all there is to say about him."[19]

The Anxieties of Maria Theresa

Maria Theresa of Austria, queen of Bohemia and Hungary, empress of Germany, champion of a theocratic ideal of power and declared enemy of Enlightenment philosophy and the French *encyclopédistes*, placed everything in the service of her politics — first and foremost her fertile body. For her, having children was a political duty. This head of state who had sixteen children, of whom ten survived, tolerated with scarcely concealed impatience the conjugal inertia of her son-in-law, Louis XVI (who, at the beginning of his marriage, regularly lay down with his wife only to fall asleep immediately, often without saying a word). The empress's correspondence with her ambassador to France reveals a clear progression in the formulation of her doubts: first, astonishment at the "timidity" of the dauphin; then, the accusation of impotence.

OCTOBER 1770: "Regarding the dauphin's state, which is disagreeable enough, I admonish my daughter to have patience and I insist that nothing is lost; but she needs to step up her caresses."

OCTOBER 1773: "And I must admit I am dying to see her pregnant now; as I cannot imagine anything is lacking on her part, it must be the dauphin."

JANUARY 1774: "The dauphin's coldness, as a young husband of twenty with a pretty wife, is inconceivable to me. Despite all the assertions of the Faculty, my suspicions are growing regarding the prince's physical constitution, and the only thing I am counting on now, really, is the intervention of the emperor, who, on reaching Versailles, may well find the means of getting such an indolent husband to acquit himself more successfully of his duty."

That same year, Maria Theresa went so far as to wish that Louis XVI's pride might be stung by the scandal sheets' declarations of his impotence And when, in 1778, Marie-Antoinette finally gave birth to a baby girl, the empress wondered "if we won't have to wait another eight years before seeing another baby."

Mme Campan, that kind soul, saw in the king's long sexual latency the effect of a bad spell. The magical figure of seven sterile years supported her contention. Less kind souls, decidedly hostile to the queen, continued to place the responsibility on Marie-Antoinette. For as long as possible (until her brother came, that is, and gave her a lesson) she had clearly shirked her conjugal duty. Bernard Faÿ is categorical: "Public opinion blamed the haughty, spendthrift queen. Her balls were becoming deserted.

She took her revenge on her husband, by refusing to give herself to him and then accusing him of impotence."[20]

Sexual Fiasco and the Decline of Etiquette

Apart from physiology, it is possible to associate the decadence of court ritual and the sexual uselessness of the king. According to the ritualistic spirit of etiquette, nothing must disturb the order of a ceremony, the prescribed words to be pronounced, the protocol to be observed. The same *Grand Siècle* spirit is found in both the seventeenth-century memorialist Saint-Simon's vision of the world and the marquis de Sade's eroticism. The unfailing loftiness of Sadian language did not allow for accident. There was no question of improvising when it came to fixed rules of behavior any more than with the rules of French grammar, and Saint-Simon and Sade played with these, too, with great virtuosity, without ever contravening them. Such rules held whether the ceremony was one of mourning or of pleasure.

At Silling Castle, in Sade's *A Hundred and Twenty Days of Sodom* (written in 1785 but not published until 1931), extreme acts were prescribed according to regulations from which one was forbidden to depart in any way. Punctuated by orgasms and evil deeds, the program of pleasure, in its formal rigor, was of the same order as a royal ceremony. The scene unfolded the way it was supposed to unfold. There was nothing to prove in anyone's eyes, especially not in the eyes of a partner. There could be no sexual fiasco (a nineteenth-century invention, like the notion of the doomed writer and the link between writing and madness).

That the last king, whose death brought the ancien régime to an end, was also the one who could not manage to ensure his descent, was not a simple coincidence. Louis XVI, who sought to flee the splendors of royal representation, the minute and constant mise-en-scène of the sacralization of the person of the king (nicely invented by Louis XIV); Louis XVI who, unlike his predecessors, never felt the slightest pleasure in being king, could not perform, with the distance and serenity of an obligatory ceremony, the act of reproduction.

Even so, the king never underestimated the importance of problems of etiquette and could even show a certain tact in this regard, as the rather delicate issue of the sex of the chevalier d'Eon reveals. Beaumarchais was sent to London on the secret mission of bringing him or her back. The court was tense with excitement. Bets on the sex of the celebrated knight reached sizable amounts. Beaumarchais himself believed, without hesitation, that Eon was a woman. His argument: "Everyone tells me that this mad woman is mad about me." And so it was as a woman that Eon was authorized to return to France. Eon's status raised a number of questions, and Beaumarchais, at the time legally stripped of his rights as a citizen, entered into direct correspondence with Louis XVI to settle them:

> Essential points that I beg M. the comte de Vergennes to present for the king's deliberation before my departure for London, on December 13, 1775, to be answered in the margin:
>
> Does the king grant permission for the damsel d'Eon to wear the cross of Saint-Louis over her ladies' clothes?
>
> *King's reply* (written in a rather shaky hand): Only out in the provinces.
>
> Does His Majesty approve the granting of 2,000 ecus, which I gave to this damsel for her maiden's trousseau?
>
> *King's reply*: Yes.
>
> In this case, does His Majesty leave entirely at her disposal all her men's garments?
>
> *King's reply*: She must sell them.

As these favors should be subject to certain dispositions to which I hope to subject the damsel d'Eon forever, would His Majesty continue to give me the authority to grant or refuse, according to what I decide is for her own good?

King's reply: Yes.[21]

The Locksmith King

The king's penchant for manual labor, locksmithing in particular, is famous. It used to infuriate Marie-Antoinette and amuse both the nobles and the people. "If he's such a good locksmith, why doesn't he, for France's sake and his own, make a chastity belt for his unfaithful better half?"[22]

Louis XVI never renounced his passion for locks, which he was still practicing at the Tuileries in the midst of great political turmoil. One morning, he told the queen, "I had a dream; it was in another century, but the doors opened and shut the same way." He stopped, for no one was listening, not even the servants.

The Lesbian Plot

As though there weren't enough to worry about with an extravagant, debauched queen transforming the court of France into a bordello and the king into an almighty cuckold. Yet it did not stop there. A further stroke of depravity was to be added: Marie-Antoinette liked women. She exhausted men without loving them. In reality, she was only interested in her own sex. The picture gets worse: what was a *frisson* of impropriety became disgust, nausea, a repulsive image. We leave to Louise Robert, a woman manifestly overwhelmed by the prospect of homosexuality, the task of accusing the queen, or rather, of interrogating her: "But can it be that Antoinette, surpassing all her like, has infected the court of France with a type of debauchery that has never before held sway there? ... My quill fails me. Antoinette! If, in your criminal hands, the state's gold has served to corrupt and seduce these miserable fools of women, to gangrene their hearts, to trample underfoot that modesty which is the foremost virtue of their sex, to transform them into vile animals, speak. Who from now on in the whole wide world could be so impure as to hear your name without shuddering in horror?"[23]

The latest scandal at Versailles under Louis XVI was that the king does not keep favorites while the queen does. (This was the reign of "such is my pleasure"; Marie-Antoinette's pleasure was for a woman.) The lesbian vice, which, they say, Marie-Antoinette inherited from her mother, made men secondary objects of the queen's lust: "if men ever dropped us, we could not be pitied," she declared to the princesse de Lamballe in one pamphlet, "for we know how to do without them."[24]

Marie-Antoinette used men out of perversity and for political ends. The *Historical Essays* depicted her as "alternately driven by her passion for women and her desire to have children." Under her influence, the "anandrine sect" ruled France and led it to sterility. "The court could not wait to follow the fashion / Every woman was both tribade and whore / No one had children anymore, which seemed convenient / Cocks were replaced by a lascivious finger."[25] And when, for political reasons, the queen wanted to have a child, rumor claims the birth will be difficult because of the "descent or collapse of the womb" produced by her unnatural morals.

The fear that homosexuality was running rampant at Versailles, that "school for dangerous women," as one pamphleteer called it, sprang from a political fear. In 1770, when Marie-Antoinette arrived in France, two powerful empires were controlled by women: Russia, under Catherine II, and Austria, under Maria Theresa. Had Marie-Antoinette shown some sense of political strategy and a keen interest in government affairs, had she revealed herself to be a woman of power, women would have had a decisive weight in the balance of international relations. Behind the fantasy of a lesbian plot lay the fear that men were losing their grip on the political reins.

The Queen's Female Lovers

Many pamphlets of the day provided lists of the queen's female lovers: Péguigny, Saint-Maigrin, Cossé, "the robust and lusty Guéménée," and so on. One of the many *Testaments of Marie-Antoinette of Austria* said: "I bequeath and leave to the young ladies d'Olivia, Soprosie, d'Arcourt, Fromenville, Julie, Bonnemont (etc., etc., etc., etc., etc., etc., etc., etc., etc., etc., etc.), for the period they served me as men, the sum of ten thousand pounds each." And in *The Testament of Marie-Antoinette, the Widow Capet* (included in this volume), the sole legacy of the queen was bequeathed to a woman: two gold rings and a lock of hair.

The vast number of Marie-Antoinette's feminine conquests recalls the women seduced and abandoned by Don Juan, whose number is sung by Leporello as "*mille e tre*," a thousand and three. Aristocrats enjoyed themselves, the servants did the accounts. This division of labor was achieved in fake complicity: an accommodating attitude with no illusions on the part of the valet; quiet cynicism on the part of the master. The eighteenth century presents a whole theater of disguises and exchanges between master and servant which usually turn, of course, to the master's advantage, since he calls the shots. But the situation was occasionally reversed; sometimes the servant fooled the master. When this occurs, lists pealed out as song or dissolve into gusts of laughter. Not so with the pamphlets' lists; they have no playful dimension. The *List of All the People with Whom the Queen Has Had Depraved Relations* (1792), for example, evinced instead the solitary excitement and maniacal attention of the voyeur. It generically approached the denunciation list of the Terror. "The thousand and one million intrigues" imputed to the "debauched queen" implied a serious sanction. Since her exploits were exemplary, her punishment should be as well.

That Messalina Polignac

Beginning in 1777, Mme de Polignac became the queen's most intimate friend and her inseparable confidante. She supplanted the princesse de Lamballe, for whom Marie-Antoinette had restored the post of superintendent of the queen's house. Even after leaving Versailles, Gabrielle Yolande Martine de Polignac would remain the uncontested favorite. Confirming this unofficial position, after the dauphin was born, the queen appointed her Governess to the Children of France (the children of the royal family). Marie-Antoinette's passionate friendship with Mme de Polignac was one of the lampoonists' favorite themes: "This sublime passion was equaled only by Louis XV's attachment to, and imbecility over, Mme de Pompadour. Like the latter, the Comtesse Jules cost the state a fortune."[26] Marie-Antoinette and Mme de Polignac represent the triumph of lesbian love. They formed an infernal couple drunkenly following the primrose path to hell. Their days and nights were given over to orgies. They had only one desire: to do ill — and they had at their disposal all the means required to do just that.

Public opinion hounded Mme de Polignac as violently as it did the queen. Polignac, however, was to be an unpunished queen of vice: the Revolution failed to make her pay for her misdeeds. Unlike the princesse de Lamballe, who had her sexual organ cut out after she was massacred (Louis-Sébastien Mercier, horrified, recounted how one man amused himself by turning it into a mustache), Mme de Polignac personifies the unconditional victory of vice.

She was one of the first to leave the court on July 16, 1789. Even though she had fled the court, the pamphleteers continued to pursue her on her adventures in Rome. Ever the nymphomaniac, she threw herself at priests, exploring every level of ecclesiastical hierarchy in her relentless lechery: "She fell into a swoon with all the urgent caresses that covered her entire body.... And thus dying up to sixty times from the extremes of limitless pleasure, she rose once again only to once again expire."[27]

Phoenix of vice, Mme de Polignac enjoyed endless orgasms during her nights in the Eternal City, while in Paris the reign of virtue was under way.

Accessories

The tribades of Versailles do not neglect artificial aids and accessories. As the duchesse de Polignac declares in one pamphlet: "If I were ambitious enough to want a little of the gods' power, it would be to make the world serve my lust."[28] But certain objects can compensate for human limitations, such as:

• Mirrors, which multiply "all the finer points of her venereal gymnastics" and proclaim her lack of modesty. "We know that even tigers seek privacy and the dark; whereas this new Laïs flaunted her obscenity and made a spectacle of those acts for which one seeks obscurity."[29]

• Dildos, which the queen and her female friends habitually used. Even during her final imprisonment, she offered her guards the following shocking exhibition: "With her right hand, the princesse de Lamballe ... foraged in her bush, which was often dripping with sweet juices. With her left hand, she masterfully and rhythmically slapped one of the royal buttocks.... They saw princesse de Lamballe pull a kind of dildo out of her pocket, which she then applied to that spot we take our joy in. It was attached with a wide ribbon, which fitted over her hips most gracefully. Mme Tourzel made her a rosette right at the small of the back. The bright scarlet ribbon contrasted beautifully with her white skin."[30]

• Miscellanea: The *Petit Journal du Palais-Royal*, which appeared in 1789, ran a column called "Furniture and Effects for Sale." The objects available are most evocative: "For sale: one superb sofa, which once served the secret pleasures of the Frotter, Jules de Polignac, who had a bed dressed in black satin, taken from renovations to the secret chamber of the Q[ueen]"; or "One magnificent bronze statue, whose peculiar structure excites the strongest admiration. It has the head of a woman, the body of a harpie, the p[rivate] parts of a female cat, the claws of an eagle, and the tail of a pig; it has been remarked that the facial features are remarkably similar to those of Q. M. A. of France"; and so on.

The paper also listed various classifieds so fantastic as to indicate a major obsession. In them one learns, for instance, that "Joseph II, emperor, brother of the queen, consumed for a number of years by a poison coursing through his veins, seeks someone to regenerate the bad blood that is choking him; he promises mountains of riches to whoever will undertake the cure. His illustrious sister is guarantor of his promise...." Elsewhere, "a pretty little squirrel with the most striking red fur you've ever seen, belonging to the queen, has just now been lost on the lawns of the Tuileries. The princess, fearing he will perish if confined, the little creature being used to the outdoors, promises fifty louis to whoever finds him."

Small wonder that so many revolutionary orators should have insisted on the need to perform a complete process of regeneration, and to create a new people. Robespierre was to assert, when discussing the institution of national holidays, "The true priest of the supreme Being is Nature — its temple is the universe, its cult virtue."[31]

The Use of Animal Metaphors

Reading only the pamphlet literature, one could be forgiven for thinking that humanity, particularly that part of humanity represented by the queen and the royalist clan, had degenerated into beasts.

Marie-Antoinette, the Unnameable, deserved the worst epithets. Running short on imagination, the lampoonist must at times have declared defeat, ostentatiously withdrawing, overwhelmed, into silence: "My quill fails me, Antoinette!" Louise Robert wrote on one of those occasions. Yes, it does happen that the lampoonist, however eloquent, however boiling over with indignation, at times could not find anything horrible enough in the available vocabulary, and felt himself incapable of fulfilling the double requirement of always naming the extremes to which vice will go, while holding a few surprises in store for the reader. But, of course, there was no question of the quill *really* failing; it must go on, continuing the tireless climb up the ladder of evil, speaking the unspeakable. To do this, if the lampoonist had any imagination, he would leave the literal behind and enjoy the illusion of waxing poetic. Naturally, he had to turn to animal metaphors to condemn the humanly inconceivable evil that the queen, Marie-Antoinette, had authored. His indignity was such that, only in abandoning the human for the animal world did he have a chance of approximating the notorious nature of the "German Shrew," "the Infernal Tyrant" — an infamous woman if ever there was one. Maintaining the noun *woman*, even within the misogynist context of most of the pamphlets, would give her too much credit: one must aim lower, reduce her to animal rank.[32]

From this claim of inhumanity, which downgraded the queen and her entourage not only from the nobility's alleged superiority, but from humanity itself, a whole repulsive and terrifying fauna surged forth, dominated by the royal pack, which was itself entirely subject to the sexual appetites of the queen. She obeyed only her instinct, which drove her to all kinds of craven acts. The animals emblematic of the vices of the queen and her favorite, the duchesse de Polignac, also known as "the female chameleon," symbolized shamelessness and depravity. For example, the queen maintained, at the state's expense, a legion of "leeches." According to the logic of "worse" proper to the pamphlets, comparison with an animal implies that the person is even more ignoble than that animal, worthy of banishment even from the world of brute beasts. The abundant use the pamphlets made of antonomasia is analogous.[33] Marie-Antoinette was Messalina, Proserpina, Frede-gond, Brunhilde, and so on; at the same time, she was unclassifiably, incomparably more criminal.

The queen, on her own, constituted the entire royal menagerie which was entirely a menagerie of ferocious beasts, except for the king, who was "timid as a hare." "The arch tigress" of Austria was frightening and had revolting morals. Animal metaphors, grafting themselves at will on her body, implied capacities for metamorphosis that were all the more fearsome for serving exclusively her hatred of the French. *The Hunt for Stinking, Ferocious Beasts, Who, After Filling Up the Woods, the Plains, etc., Have Spread to the Court and the Capital* (1789), depicted her as a panther. She headed the list of "carnivorous and venomous animals" whose dead carcasses fetched top price. This pamphlet's first article, in the form of hunting rules, stipulated: "We are thoroughly convinced that a female panther, having escaped from the court of Germany, has remained in France for several years without wreaking havoc ... but for some time now, she has regained all her German rage. Let's fix her death at forty thousand livres. She is strong, powerful, has inflamed eyes, and sports red hair...." In the same pamphlet, Mme de Polignac was a barbarous she-wolf who had copulated with the red female panther and a prodigious number of animals of different species. Rabid, she had the run of the country. Her capture and death would fetch twenty thousand livres.

The presentation of Marie-Antoinette as a ferocious animal corresponds to the contempt the queen was alleged to feel for the people. She became an animal because, from the start, she considered the French to be animals. She treated others like dogs. *The Amorous Soirees of General Mothier* [sic] *and the Beautiful Antoinette, by the Austrian Woman's Little Spaniel* (1791) denounced the arrogance of the queen's whims: she adopted people and dropped them at will. The little dog, until then adored by his mistress, has just been replaced by General Motier (Lafayette): "I was everything, now I'm nothing," he wails. In a similar situation, ignored by a Venetian aristocrat whom he can't manage to seduce, Casanova cried out: "I was nothing, it was too much!" It is worth emphasizing here that the abandoned spaniel *talked*, an exceptional phenomenon in the bestiary of the pamphlets. He was given a voice because he enjoyed the pamphleteer's sympathy, and his voice, the voice of morality or of the victim, accorded with public opinion. Conversely, when animal metaphors were applied to enemies of the people, they produced dumb animals with whom it was not possible to communicate. The only goal was to track them down and to slaughter them.

Surrounding the arch tigress (herself the product of a union between a female monkey and a tiger or a bear) there appeared a crowd of mute animals, the spider her daughter, the wolf Polignac, the pig Louis XVI, the fox Provence, and her entire court of monkeys, owls, stone martens, tawny owls, crows — are we witnessing a revival of La Fontaine's fable world, with its endless mobility between man and animal, its unresolvable ambiguity? Not at all. The bestiary of the pamphlets has nothing in common with La Fontaine's fables, where reciprocal desires and identities circulate between man and animal. Lions fall in love with shepherdesses, and their attentions are not unwelcome: "For besides, in any case / The Beauty liked ferocious folk / A girl will gladly take on / Lovers with long mane."[34] In contrast, the animals caged in the Tuileries, or on the run in France or abroad, were not described for the pleasure of fantasy. They were merely catalogued, and their incarnation as various animals, all of them pests, was not offered as an imaginative exercise but as the revelation of their hidden natures: the pamphlets warned that the human appearance of the king, the queen, and the aristocracy was a trap.

The animal metamorphoses so common in the pamphlets, however outrageous and improbable, were profoundly realistic. They were reality at last exposed. Gérard Genette writes of the poet Saint-Amant's bestiary that it is "composed almost exclusively of birds and fish: a predilection in keeping with the most obvious characteristics of the Baroque soul, which seeks and projects itself in the fleeting and the unobtainable."[35] He adds: "Through the bird-fish metaphor, a much broader theme is thus proposed, that of the reversibility of the world and of existence."[36] It is telling, then, that there were no fish in the animal world of the pamphlets and generally few birds (and the few there are were not selected for their ability to fly). Here we are dealing with land animals who belong to a fixed universe where there is no floating or flight. Their ugly, terrifying forms indicate the irreversibility of combat, the inexpiable nature of hate.

Comtesse Valois de La Motte

Woe betide the victims of these ferocious beasts! One of the most illustrious was the comtesse Valois de La Motte. Opposite the queen, Polignac, and all those depraved women who treated the world as a store of accessories for the perfection of their orgasms, Mme de La Motte played the role of virtuous victim. She was the Justine of the prerevolutionary epic.

This young adventuress, who initially managed to draw attention to herself by going regularly to court to faint, achieved fame
with the scandal over the queen's diamond necklace. She was
accused of serving as intermediary between the queen and Cardinal de Rohan, who was allegedly in love with the countess.
Among the many pamphlets devoted to her, several stand out: the
Memoirs in Defense of comtesse Valois de La Motte Written by herself
(London, 1788) as well as the *Second Memoirs in Defense of comtesse de Valois de La Motte* (London, 1789), and there is also the
anonymous *The Queen Unmasked, or Supplement to the Memoirs of
comtesse Valois de La Motte* (London, 1789).

These monotonous, laborious speeches for the defense, punctuated by "I have already said" and "as will be recalled," were undaunted by repetition. What they defend can be summed up in a
few words: "I need to prove that my existence has been nothing
but a string of more or less extreme ordeals, which, in reality, is
rather true."[37] After an auspicious beginning not unrelated to her
charm and daring, Mme de La Motte suffered a few serious set-
backs. At the close of the Diamond Necklace trial, she took all the
blame. She was condemned to be branded with a red-hot iron,
while Cardinal de Rohan and Cagliostro were cheered in the
brightly lit streets of Paris, the night they were released. Mme de
La Motte later sought exile in England and died in London, either
by throwing herself or being thrown from her window, just as the
revolutionaries were preparing her return to France to testify at
the queen's trial. Her death precluded the testimony that might
have reversed her fortunes.

The Diamond Necklace Affair and the ensuing trial were symp-
toms of the unanimous hatred of the queen. All the characters
mixed up in it became popular heroes as an indirect result. Cagliostro hardly needed the extra publicity. In 1785 he was at the
peak of his glory. He and his wife, Serafina, had a real cult follow-

ing, the faithful coming from all walks of life and wearing fans, brooches, and hats decorated with effigies of the magic couple. Innocent though these fads may be, their spread nonetheless coincided exactly with increasing promulgation, by the enlightened, of prophecies of revolution. This is why, according to Louis Massignon, Marie-Antoinette's fall, having begun with the scandal sheet campaign, was continued by the maneuvers of the visionaries and charlatans with whom her contemporaries were so infatuated.

The flat, blasphemous pornography of the pamphlets complemented the practices of the visionaries and their otherworldly messages: both attacked royalty by divine right and especially the queen, who, unlike Louis XVI, could not conceive of any other form of government, because she knew where her interests lay (she happily subscribed to her brother Joseph II's declaration: "I'm a royalist, that's my job"), because her vision of the world was entirely tied up with her religious education, because intellectual curiosity, in political or other matters, was not her cup of tea. The queen was clearly the dragon to slay. Mobilized against her were the ambitious schemers who wanted the king's seat, idealists building a new era, and false prophets making fables of the future. Massignon writes, with his usual paradoxical lucidity:

The original lampoonists, procured for Provence and Orléans, were reinforced by unrepentant recidivists, a reverse "foreign legion" of secret crime, magnetizers, "mesmerizers," ill-intentioned occultists. In 1793, they launched *Le Père Duchesne* and Operation Agrippina (incest) against the queen to finally polish her off. In 1785, to get the king to lock her up in disgust and have her strangled, it was Operation Messalina in Suburra. "Comte de Cagliostro" (Joseph Balsamo) was chosen for the job. That dark figure from *The Arabian*

Nights, a Maltese Arab claiming to be the son of a muslim woman related to the sharif of Mecca and brought up by the mufti of Medina, was, in reality, no more than a professional pimp (for his own wife), got up as a worldly fakir.[38]

While Massignon (who is unusual in interpreting the Revolution as the revenge of the Templars and in giving secret sects a decisive role in it) sees Cagliostro as the key figure in the Diamond Necklace Affair, the scandal sheets of the day cast the comtesse de La Motte in the starring role, no doubt because, in the battle of women that pits her against Marie-Antoinette, she was the victim of the state's injustice or of the queen's seduction (which were one and the same thing). In her plaintive "autobiography," La Motte told how she came to fall prey to the libertine queen, who wickedly initiated her into Sapphic pleasures. La Motte recounts a midnight rendezvous at the Petit Trianon: "At last she appeared. Heavens! I found her so beautiful! . . . I said to myself: It is the goddess Flora, toying with a humble little flower."[39] Indeed. The little flower is soon supplanted, for the goddess is already gathering nectar elsewhere. La Motte laments, "Oh! Women! Women! Especially princesses and worst of all queens! She writes to me as though I'm a valet — so dry, so arid. . . ."[40]

The hapless heroine of the cardinal's trial, the "penitent from the shores of the Seine," has defined the enemy, enemies rather, through whom vice triumphs and is transmitted: the line of criminal queens.

The Bloodthirsty Woman

The pamphlets against Marie-Antoinette, linking sexual fantasies with political animosities, did not invent any new themes. They merely borrowed the tried and true themes of a long tradition of discourses, songs, and caricatures levied against women in power —

particularly foreign women, whether Anne of Austria or Marie de' Medici. Marie-Antoinette differed from her predecessors only in that the Revolution translated the violence of these fantasies into action; the blood was real blood.

Marie-Antoinette loved blood. She was a dissolute queen and a criminal queen. Blasé about simple pleasures, she recharged her erotic energy by dreaming up criminal schemes against the French people. For this perverse woman, sexual appetite amounted to a taste for revenge. Marie-Antoinette, bloodthirsty and a nymphomaniac: the two charges are indistinguishable. In the arms of the swarthy Polignac, the blond, the russet, the ruddy Antoinette found relief from the fatigues of lovemaking in dreaming of the destruction of her subjects. The bloodbath was one of the great royal pleasures. The massacre of the French (described by "the Austrian Woman" in the pamphlets as "frogs of the Seine") will be the climax of that long orgy with which her life is identified. "My sole desire," the sovereign proclaims, "is to see this capital bathed in its own blood.... Each French head, when presented to me, will be paid its weight in gold."[41] Much as coconuts, the skulls would serve as cups. "Fatigued by our pleasures, drained with exhaustion, we paused only to jeer at the misery of the public and to drink deeply from the cup of crime. The potion filling it portended that soon, like Caligula, we would be drinking the blood of Frenchmen from it, and *in their own skulls* — a barbarous refinement with which antiquity has furnished us more than one example."[42]

These rivers, these torrents, these oceans of blood into which Marie-Antoinette dreamed of plunging herself were the apparent manifestation of her murderous lust. But she had more than one string to her deadly bow. She also knew the art of poisoning, the traditional arm of feminine wiles. One of the recurrent themes of this literature was that of the poisoner queen. She was accused of having poisoned Maurepas, Vergennes ("I got hold of the recipe of Marie de' Medici"[43]), Mirabeau ("I would say the poison that killed Mirabeau was distilled in her own mortar"[44]), and her own son, the dauphin, who died on June 4, 1789 ("She thus set to work and herself distilled the juice brought to Colchis by the famous Medea. The poor constitution of the dauphin was grist to Marie-Antoinette's mill."[45]). It goes without saying that she tried to poison Louis XVI. *The Degeneration of the Royal Blood and the Poisoning of Louis XVI King of the French* (1791) caught Marie-Antoinette in the act of serving her husband "a lethal dose of crushed diamonds, subtlely and finely infused in the royal coffee pot." The same pamphlet addressed the "weak and unhappy king": "Your slow and painful death will serve as an example to all potentates, snug in the caresses of their wives; your Antoinette has dug your grave and your Levites — those imposters — want to revive the unhappy century of the League."

Frivolous, extravagant, libertine, orgiastic, lesbian, incestuous, and bloodthirsty, a poisoner and an infanticide, Marie-Antoinette tried her hand at every crime. Through her wickednesses she caused the Revolution. She ruined the country, brought the people to despair, drove them to revolt: "All must be revealed, it was from your lechery / That our coffers were emptied to pay for your pleasures" charges *The Cause of the French Revolution, or the Secret Conduct of Marie-Antoinette of Austria, Queen of France* (1790). After having brought about the fall of the ancien régime, she struggled to preserve it. She was corruption personified, infinitely decadent.

In order to counter the scourge of the century, the Revolution produced chaste and pure heroes: Robespierre was known as "the Incorruptible," while Saint-Just, aptly named, was a sober, archangelic young man, whose legislative plans for republican institutions gave priority to the education of children ("children should neither be struck nor fondled") and affection between (male) friends. Saint-Just indulged the utopia of a virgin, virile world, in which women have no role whatsoever. They are so nonexistent that they cannot even be censured. The world belongs to "friends" who, without touching or speaking, lavish on each other the signs of fidelity: "Friends stand by each other in combat. Friends over a lifetime are placed in the same grave. Friends go into mourning for each other. Friends dig each other's grave, make each other's funeral arrangements, and along with children, strew flowers on each other's burial place."[46]

These knights of Good preferred death to submission to the female demon. They could face the Gorgon's head without trembling. With the courage of Oedipus before the Sphinx, or Saint George before the dragon, they resolved to slay the Monster.

Infernal tyrant, scourge of the universe, Marie-Antoinette was utterly inhuman: "Her callous eyes, treacherous and inflamed, radiate sheer fire and carnage to gratify her craving for unjust revenge; her nose and cheeks are purple and poxy from the rotten blood that seeps between her flesh and her already leaden hide, and her fetid, stinking mouth harbors a cruel tongue, eternally thirsty for French blood!"[47]

All the heads guillotined under the Revolution were so many multiplications of the Hydra-Antoinette. She must die (but is this possible, since a new head springs forth with each decapitation?) for the reign of purity to begin.

It is out of self-defense that the Revolution spilled blood. It was out of depravity that Marie-Antoinette craved it and seduced her supporters into following the example of her cruelty. The queen's perversity demanded bloodshed, it made the Revolution bloody: "The blood spilled from 1789 to September 1792 was her doing, with her intrigues and her mad passion to have the French destroy themselves."[48] She breathed the spirit of discord. In her, the slow death rattle of a society and its refusal to die were simultaneously incarnated. She had brought about the end of the old world; now she opposed the birth of the new.

She was not only the cause of all misfortune, but its absolute origin. She was indistinguishable from her womb, that devouring pit, that vessel of poison, vast enough to supply the world — or, at least, all the armies of the counterrevolution: "Since the Revolution, the monarchist club, whose body and soul is Antoinette, have been continually at it; all its members have drawn from the vagina of the Austrian Woman the poison it is hard at work distilling. That infectious cavern is the receptacle of all vices, where each comes and takes his required dose."[49]

The Bleeding Marie-Antoinette

The queen revealed herself to be a woman and impure to the very end. In the final months of her captivity she suffered interminable periods. Prey to constant bleeding, she stained her clothes and did not have enough linen to staunch the flow.

If the Revolution represents the masculine principle, the queen embodies the feminine principle. The bloody standard of her red hair is also the emblem of the religion of menstruation.

A people is without honor and deserves its chains when it bows down before the Scepter of Queens.

CHAPTER FIVE

Chant of Loathing

The Battle of Origins

The pornography inspired by Marie-Antoinette attained such intensity because it went hand in hand with a delirium about inception. It became a matter of setting against the "German Shrew" — born of evil and perpetrating it — another procreative force: virtuous republican maternity, which all Frenchwomen must take upon themselves. "Couples who produce no children in the first seven years of marriage, and who have adopted none, are separated by law and must part," a law put forward by Saint-Just stipulated. (Note that Saint-Just himself fell under the spell of the same magical number that kept Marie-Antoinette and Louis XVI infertile for the first seven years of their marriage!)

Marie-Antoinette engendered discord, exuded poison. Her womb was pestilential. Bolts of lightning darted from her eyes. She was born of the mists of time, but also, more seriously, of *another woman*. Beyond Marie-Antoinette stretched the whole terrifying line of "dangerous women"[1] — cruel, wanton, ravaging queens, wicked mothers, repositories of all the vices. Maria Theresa belonged indisputably to this race.

Inhabited by satanic forces, Maria Theresa has sworn to perpetuate them. The role played by the empress in the opinion campaign against her daughter is that of prime cause. Through her, one comes much closer to the source of evil. The poison of the monarchy was concocted in the vagina of the Austrian Woman, but she was simply her mother's daughter. Maria Theresa's conception of Marie-Antoinette stemmed from a desire for revenge. She sought to propagate not life but destruction. In opposition to the maternity of salvation represented in Catholicism by the Virgin Mary and resurrected in revolutionary ideology by the urgent appeal to populate the fatherland, there was — the pamphlets lead one to believe — a maternity of revenge perpetuating the royal family and inflicting suffering and perdition on the people, who were its victim. The birth of Marie-Antoinette satisfied Maria Theresa's horror of humanity and of the French in particular: "What a perfect revenge on this nation for me to give it such a monster," she gloated.[2]

Louis XVI's wife was the daughter of crime, and when she finally managed to become a mother, it was only to consummate this fatal lineage: "A daughter of crime, I now give birth to it in turn; I am a monster abhorred throughout nature, and wherever the Supreme Being may place you rejoice, Mother, rejoice in my criminal labors."[3]

This criminal filiation in the service of the monarchy (identified with the sovereignty of feminine pleasure), was accomplished in dark, putrid caverns: feudal castles, witches' lairs, the womb of depraved queens. It was combated by the good maternity. This "superhuman maternity," as Michelet called it, was dedicated to the salvation of the nation, to the birth of a regenerated humanity. It has its heroines: for example, citizen Marcier, who "gave birth to a girl whose left breast bears a bonnet of liberty [Phrygian cap] *prominently* and *in color....*" This curious event, as a journalist commented, proves not only that nature had set its seal of approval on the reign of independence, but testifies further to the close attachment that the mother of this child feels for the sacred signs of liberty.

The heroines of this truly republican, "superhuman" maternity in fact served a masculine principle, as Lynn Hunt observes: "The nation, Paris, and the Revolution were all good mothers; Marie-Antoinette was the bad mother. It should be noted, however, that the nation, Paris, and the Revolution were motherly in a very abstract, even nonfeminine fashion (in comparison to Marie-Antoinette)."[4]

Through her odious fecundity, the queen transmitted the germs of a perverse femininity, inherited from her own mother. The germs transmitted by Maria Theresa to her daughter were all the more pernicious because they were invisible, especially since malignancy has raged since ancient times. Worthy offspring of the "clever empress," Marie-Antoinette was merely the last of a long line of wicked queens, each driven by a fiercely competitive spirit to outdo the exploits of her predecessor.

Marie-Antoinette lived forever in the shadow of Maria Theresa, but their comparison has more than one dimension. It comprises a whole series of perverse queens, toward whom the pamphlets adopted an official tone of malediction, but with a force of repetition that reveals secret gratification. These heinous, sexually abandoned women offered consolation for the austerities of the cult of virtue, for its terrible radiance.

In opposition to the broad daylight of liberty proclaimed (prominently and in color), the wicked queens cast night shadows. The more they are condemned, the more they return.

Into a Frightful Cavern

A dream attributed to Marie-Antoinette put into play the obsession with the feminine cavern, of the female demonism that the queen, strengthened by her absolute power over the king and his people, incarnated without constraint. In this dream, Marie-Antoinette communicates with the evil women of the past through her mother: "I found myself carried by my mother into a frightful cavern...."[5]

In this dark and horrible place her illustrious predecessors appeared before her. One by one they addressed her to steel her resolve. Fredegond, the first, recalled her triumphs:

> "They watched as I led the soldiers to victory, with my son in my arms, and set for all peoples the example of a woman who can fight and win. Look at my life. Have I not made it clear that, in order to hold the reins of absolute power, one must not rely on petty means? Necessity, the circumstances, justify all; besides, if we weigh the people down a little with our scepter, we are merely punishing them for having removed us from a throne we could have occupied just as well as our idiot husbands. Go forward, Antoinette, do not stop in the middle of your career. It is through dauntless courage that we accomplish the hardest feats." At these words, I felt the earth shake beneath me and a whirlwind hid Fredegond from sight, but she was soon replaced by a young woman dressed in white....[6]

This is Judith of Bavaria, wife of Louis the Debonair, a magnificent bitch. Come to admonish the queen, she enjoined her not to deviate from her policy of doing her worst to obtain her ends, and concluded: "'You see, Antoinette, one must not renounce the schemes one has conceived....' Judith disappeared and I saw Isabeau of Bavaria, Eleonore, the wife of Charles VIII, and finally, the celebrated Catherine de' Medici. Isabeau said to me: 'We know how distraught you are, Antoinette; you have done all you can to follow in our footsteps, but your stupid husband wrecks everything your genius and mastery have devised; but take courage, women like us do not lack it. They reproach you with being a little debauched, the people are starting to talk; let them hiss their complaints, they can't harm you...."[7] Catherine de' Medici had the final say, addressing the terrorized queen with these words: "'Spare nothing ... let rivers of blood flow.... Deceit, betrayal — you need these more than ever....'" "At these words," says Antoinette, "swirls of flames and smoke arose in that awful place.... I can still see those hideous specters...."[8]

Fredegond, Judith, Isabeau, Eleonore, Catherine de' Medici. Their example is further blackened by the equally deplorable deeds of Anne of Austria, Cleopatra, Messalina, the queen of the Amazons, Basina (the queen of Thuringia), Brunhilde (who, with her own bare hands, crushed her great-grandson against a wall), Plectrude the Opinionated, Richilde, specialist in gratuitous crime, Constance, Bertrade, Eleonore (the one whose debauchery gave gangrene to an entire army during the Crusades), Anne de Beaujeu, Anne de Bretagne, Louise de Savoie, Marie de' Medici (in whom Italian and German blood mingled), Clotilda, Blanche de Castille (who behaved toward her son, Saint Louis, "like Nero's mother"), and Proserpina. All these women are cited, outside any historical reference, in the atemporality of crime, the eternity of hell. As with Elagabulus, historians wanting to recount their lives come up against "an impossible chronology," an unimaginable interweaving of "dateless crimes."[9] These dead princesses and queens, the scandalous memory of whom dares to rival the renown of great men — such as the heroes of ancient Greece or republican Rome so often invoked during the Revolution — shared a notoriety that their misdeeds and open contempt for their husbands have earned for them. But even among such evil company, Marie-Antoinette stood out as supremely wicked.

In the course of a strained conversation, two queens of the worst reputation, Fredegond and Catherine de' Medici, admitted that they were outshone by this newcomer, Maria Theresa's daughter. "Prove to me by authentic facts and irreproachable witnesses," said Catherine de' Medici, at first sceptical that anyone could outdo her own evil deeds (so proud is she of the massacre of Saint Bartholomew), "that Antoinette of Austria really is the wickedest and vilest of all."[10] Fredegond, made ruthless by her own defeat, exhorted Catherine to be humble. She must bow to Antoinette: "It requires only a brief perusal of Antoinette's life to realize that her heart, far from harboring the slightest virtue, is the repository of all the vices. Incest, adultery, the most lewd and culpable lechery, the reversal of the sacred order of nature were all just games to this shameless Messalina."[11] Then Fredegond, murderous wife of Chilperic, delivered the decisive judgment: "Having outdone us, she had to outdo herself. Ordinary crimes no longer satisfied her bloodthirsty, ferocious soul...."[12]

This praise, however grudging, pronounced by the paragons of crime, made Marie-Antoinette the Incomparable, the Unnameable. In the sphere in which she reigned, no matter how ferocious the queens who were her role models, she did not suffer comparison: "She does not have her like here."[13]

From Marie-Antoinette of Lorraine-Austria to Antoinette of Austria: The Elimination of Paternal Ancestry

Baptized "Marie-Antoine Josèphe Johanna," the child was called Antoine for the first years of her life, in the court of Vienna. On her arrival in France, she became "Marie-Antoinette."

In their disrespectfully familiar, then hostile style, the scandal sheets played havoc with the queen's name. The diminutives "Antoinette," "Toinette," and "Toinon" might seem affectionate if the context in which they were used did not belie the least amicable feeling. During such a deeply religious age, the dropping of "Marie" was pointedly insulting and degrading, imputing that the queen was unworthy of bearing the Virgin's name.

Marie-Anne-Charlotte Corday (almost always referred to as

Charlotte Corday), the murderer of the Montagnard journalist of Marat, was a monster that posters on walls everywhere depicted as "a virago more fleshy than fresh, graceless and dirty, like all female philosophers and fine minds." She too had her virginal Christian name amputated. "Marie" was her favorite name as a girl, the one she always signed.

The abbreviation of these women's names by revolutionary justice (during her trial, Marie-Antoinette was always called Antoinette) symbolically prefigured the foreshortening of their bodies by the guillotine.

In the course of her battles with French public opinion, the queen lost not only the protection of the Virgin but her patrilineal heritage. Once referred to as Marie-Antoinette of Lorraine-Austria (her father, Francis I, had been duke of Lorraine), she becomes simply Antoinette of Austria. Any reference to her father, who linked her, by birth, to France, is dropped.

Antoinette of Austria was her mother's daughter. There was never any allusion to her father. The legend of the wicked queen — instrument of vengeance of the Empress of Austria, who is the condensation of feminine vice and henchwoman of all who hate the French — entailed the complete effacement of Francis I, Maria Theresa's seductive and beloved husband. Francis I, duc de Lorraine, always remained passionately attached to his native soil. He was not Austrian and never became so — which is why he had to be erased from all the imaginary biographies of Marie-Antoinette produced by the lampoonists. Francis I had to disappear so that the paternal lineage of the Foreign Woman could be ignored — that genealogical line that linked her to the French kings Henry IV and Saint Louis. (It is worth noting here that Francis I's mother, Elisabeth-Charlotte d'Orléans, wife of Léopold-Josèphe de Lorraine and sister of the regent Philippe d'Orléans, was the daughter of Louis XIV's brother and the princesse Palatine.)

The duke was a native of Lorraine and a libertine freemason, passionately interested in music and the theater; his dynasty was descended in the fifteenth century from René d'Anjou. Through her father, the Austrian Woman is, in reality, one of the most French queens in the history of France. But myth takes from reality only what it can use. The rest might as well not exist.

Camille Desmoulins's Prohibition

The queen of France was a monster. The discourse of the pamphlets kept harking back to the extent of her depravity. This dirge never ended, since what caused it — and what it repudiated — was the persistent belief in the queen's sanctity. This chant of loathing rejected the sanctity that it derided and yet on which it thrived. One never got tired of insulting Marie-Antoinette because each insult elicited a shiver of blasphemy, the thrill of heaping trash on the sacred. The energy required to repeat these litanies of vice, to continually cover the same ground, could never be exhausted — so long as the idea persisted of a distinct, superior, inconceivable essence in the mysterious being of a queen.

As early as 1789, the lawyer and journalist Camille Desmoulins, founder of the *Revolutions of France and Brabant*, tried in vain to put a stop to the rage of desecration which he found alien to the true republican spirit. Desmoulins understood that such desecration was endless by definition, that it would never run out of epithets, because there is always *worse*. The only way to silence the blasphemous discourse of the French, Desmoulins believed, would be to strip the queen's name of its gloss, so that it could no longer induce fear and trembling, the secret desire to prostrate oneself. And if the word "queen" cannot be desanctified (since all the deformations and mutilations to which it is subject fail to dispel the magic), at least one could try to ban the word — which is what Desmoulins demanded in his journal:

If ever there was an astonishing pair of words, it is *Queen of the French*. Russia, England, Hungary, and Sweden can have queens, but what has always distinguished the Franks is that they do not have one. There cannot be a *Queen of the French*: the Salic Law is categorical. Marie-Antoinette of Austria is the wife of the king, and nothing more.... I am not unaware that our fathers said Queen Catherine de' Medici, Queen Isabelle of Bavaria, and in distant times, Queen Brunhilde, Queen Fredegond, without meaning to contravene the Salic Law. I find the term to be merely a formality, like that expression at the end of a letter, "Your humble servant." *But it is with words that men are governed.* Can there be any doubt that it was this word that put the notion into these women's heads that they were the executive power and not simply the procreative power? ... I thus move the motion that it be forbidden in public records to use the term *Queen of the French,* as it is contrary to the Salic Law, ringing oddly in the ear of patriots, and reeking of servitude.[14]

But Desmoulins's proscription, like any other ban on language, could not escape the logic of linguistic negation, which implies the affirmation of that which it excludes. In proscribing "Queen of the French," he too was obliged to intone the dirge of the accursed queens. "Blasphemy," Emile Benveniste observes, "is entirely a process of speech; it consists, in a sense, of replacing the name of God by its violation."[15] To forbid blasphemy, to proscribe the transgression of a taboo and the pleasure thus derived, is still to acknowledge the power of that taboo, to affirm the sacred aura of a name.

Desmoulins's resolution had no effect. Right up to Marie-Antoinette's execution, the pamphleteers continued to catalog her crimes and to blaspheme the *name* of Queen. For, when Vice has lost its prestige, what sacrifice can be offered to Virtue?

The Widow Capet

When it came to the queen's trial, the passions aroused by images of the Infernal Woman remained unabated, long having exceeded the bounds of credibility. The baroque incantation of the pamphlets, the lyricism of the Queen of Evil's saga, continued to function throughout the brisk succession of questions and answers and the stock phrases of the interrogation.

Hébert's statement attested to the persistence of the myth:

> Finally, the young Capet [the king's son], whose health was deteriorating daily, was surprised by Simon in an act of self-abuse, fatal for his condition; when the latter enquired who had taught him this criminal ruse, he replied that he owed his familiarity with the fatal habit to his mother and his aunt. The witness declares that from the statement made by the young Capet, in the presence of the mayor of Paris and the prosecutor of the Commune, it appears the two women often made him sleep between them; that acts of the most unbridled debauchery were committed there; that there is no doubt, from what Capet's son has said, that an act of incest was committed between mother and son.[16]

The judgment of Marie-Antoinette, her condemnation, and her execution unfolded in the theater of crime, upon whose stage, where she strutted her insatiable sexuality and diabolical perversity, she was the uncontested heroine.

But the order of the day was commonness: the queen's name was forbidden. The person allegedly called to appear before the justice of the people was not Proserpina nor Messalina (still less the queen of the Amazons followed by her band of female warriors with their breasts cut off) but merely the widow Capet. As the historian Daniel Arasse writes, "the death of the queen follows a logic arising from the decision of September 5, 1793, by which the Terror was made the order of the day: at war with the monarchies of Europe, the Revolution must eliminate its enemies who, from the inside, offer support (however inoffensive) to the foreign party; thus Marie-Antoinette is convicted of intelligence with the enemy and accordingly executed, no longer as the queen of France, but as the widow Capet. Her death must be ordinary and thereby confirm the established existence of the Republic, which no longer has any need for founding sacrifices."[17]

The trial, like the ritual of execution, tried to tidy away "the widow Capet" under common law. Whereas Louis XVI had been judged by the Convention, Marie-Antoinette appeared before the revolutionary tribunal like any other suspect citizen. The president of the tribunal declared: "A woman formerly surrounded by the most splendid privileges that the pride of kings and the servility of slaves could invent, today occupies, at the nation's court, the place occupied by another woman two days ago, and this equality ensures her a fair trial." But, despite such declarations of principle, the exceptional nature of the accused never stopped being taken into account, giving a unique dimension to supposedly egalitarian measures.

The trial began on October 15, 1793, at eight o'clock in the morning, and finished the next day at four-thirty in the morning. At dawn, after debating before the convention, the jury declared Marie-Antoinette guilty on all counts submitted to their deliberation.[18] "Antoinette, here is the jury's declaration..." After those words, "Antoinette" listened to the public prosecutor Fouquier-Tinville's closing speech and, finally, the verdict condemning her: "The tribunal, following the unanimous declaration of the jury, and acceding to the closing speech of the public prosecutor according to the laws cited by him, condemns said Marie-Antoinette, known as Lorraine of Austria, widow of Louis Capet, to the death penalty; declares that, in conformity with the law of March 10 last, her belongings, if she has any on French soil, be acquired and confiscated for the benefit of the Republic; and orders that, at the public prosecutor's request, the present sentence be executed at the Place de la Révolution, and published and advertised throughout the Republic."

The game was lost. Throughout her twenty-hour trial, she played her part well, with intelligence and skill, driven by the desire to win — because she wanted to live, but also, perhaps, because for once, for the first and last time in her existence as "the wife of the king," she alone had been addressed. As the widow Capet, she was no longer anyone's wife. She could speak and lie in her own name.

She was taken to the "chamber of the condemned" in the *conciergerie* for the brief period separating her from her execution. Dazed by fatigue, she could not make out her surroundings. She kept hearing voices, her own among them, powerless, far away. She said her prayers, slept for a short while, and ate something, so as not to faint. She prepared herself carefully, in mind as much as in body. As requested, she had removed her mourning clothes, considered too impressive, and put on white. She wore black stockings and elegant shoes in black silk — sole surviving indices of past luxury.

While she was preparing to die, the capital was preparing for war. The Convention was rallying. At seven o'clock, Paris was ready to wipe out any possible royalist insurrection. Patrols covered the streets, cannons were positioned on the squares and bridges. Excessive prudence and precaution? Perhaps. But more importantly, Paris, thus armed, showed itself to be a match for the destructive force that Marie-Antoinette, symbolically, represented.

Very early on, the crowd rushed to the route the condemned woman was to follow. The Place de la Révolution was swarming with people. To pass the time while they waited, the people ate,

drank, chatted. Chortling, they read out loud the most pornographic passages from the latest scandal sheets against her: *The
Queen's Farewells to her Sweethearts, Male and Female*; *Marie-
Antoinette's Great Disease* or *The Testament of Marie-Antoinette,
the Widow Capet*. At last she arrived, hands tied, sitting straight-
backed on the seat in the executioner's cart. Unlike Louis XVI, who
had been carried to the scaffold in a closed coach, she mounted
"with bravado" the "carriage with thirty-six doors" — like everyone else. A hedgerow of soldiers on either side of her passage
prevented acts of violence against her. The slowness of the cart
(which took an hour to get from the Conciergerie to the Place de
la Révolution) delighted and exasperated spectators impatient for
her to die, but who savored her humiliation. Marie-Antoinette
did not bat an eye at the hissing and booing that measured her
path. She descended nimbly from the cart and, on the scaffold,
helped the executioner speed up her own execution. "The bitch
was daring and insolent to the very end," Hébert observed.

Her execution provoked demonstrations of joy. "Long live the
Republic! Long live Liberty!" Women cried out: "They've often
told us about hell and the devil; her head has just fallen. The devil
is no more." Such was the first day of Paradise. There had to be
singing, dancing, flying over the trees in the Tuileries gardens.
And no splashing about in the Gorgon's black blood.

"The devil is no more," the women repeated; but they were
unable to move. They continued to stare — without seeing — at
the outstretched body of the headless queen.

Notes

EPIGRAPH

1. Roland Barthes, *Mythologies*, trans. Annette Lavers (New York: Noonday Press, 1990), p. 110.

INTRODUCTION

1. Chantal Thomas, *L'Oeil de la lettre* (Paris: Payot, 1978) and *Sade* (Paris: Seuil, 1994). All translations are the translator's, unless otherwise noted.

2. Chantal Thomas, *Casanova, un voyage libertin* (Paris: Denoël, 1985; Gallimard Folio, 1998).

3. Contrary to what Peter Nagy describes in *Libertinage et révolution* (Paris: Gallimard, 1975), revolutionary freedom based on community and duty and the asocial and immoral libertine license based on the desires of the moment are in complete opposition: this is what the works of Crébillon fils and Laclos, and Vivant Denon's *No Tomorrow* demonstrate. For a more profound and subtle understanding of the libertine world see: *The Libertine Reader: Eroticism and Enlightenment in Eighteenth-Century France*, ed. Michel Feher (New York: Zone Books, 1997).

4. See in particular Robert Darnton, *The Literary Underground of the Old Regime* (Cambridge, MA: Harvard University Press, 1982) and *Edition et Sédition: L'Univers de la littérature clandestine au XVIIIe siècle* (Paris: Gallimard, 1991).

5. See also J. P. Belin, *Le Commerce des livres prohibés à Paris de 1750 à 1789* (New York: B. Franklin, 1962 [1913]).

6. Hector Fleischmann, *Le Cénacle libertin de Mlle Rancourt* (Paris: Bibliothèque des Curieux, 1912), p. 3.

7. See Christian Jouhaud, *Mazarinades: La Fronde des mots* (Paris: Aubier, 1985) and for a more general and linguistic approach see Marc Angenot, *La Parole pamphlétaire: Typologie des discours modernes* (Paris: Payot, 1982).

8. Philippe Roger, *Roland Barthes, roman* (Paris: Le Livre de Poche, Biblio Essais, 1990), p. 112.

9. Roland Barthes, *Mythologies*, trans. Annette Lavers (New York: Hill and Wang, 1972), p. 109.

10. *Ibid.*, p. 11.

11. *Ibid.*, p. 143.

12. *Ibid.*, p. 147.

13. The genre of *vie privée* [private life], situated between biography and pamphlet, offers the reader a tale in which the choice of anecdotes and the interpretations of the lives of famous people are extremely biased. The implicit contract between the author and his public is that the latter enters the intimate (and necessarily scandalous) lives of the heros and heroines.

14. The Riding School at Paris was near the Tuileries and served as the meeting place for the National Assembly.

15. See Lynn Hunt, *Eroticism and the Body Politic* (Baltimore: Johns Hopkins University Press, 1991) and *The Family Romance of the French Revolution* (Berkeley: University of California Press, 1992).

16. We might add narcissistic and morbid, considering the way Saint-Just celebrated the cult of male friendship.

17. "Men made July 14, women October 6," writes Michelet in *Les Femmes de la révolution* (Paris: H. Delattays, 1854).

18. *Ibid.*, p. 27.

19. *Ibid.*, p. 22. On the question of female heroism during the revolution see Chantal Thomas, "Heroism in the Feminine: The Examples of Charlotte Corday and Madame Roland," in *The French Revolution, 1789-89: Two Hundred Years*

of Rethinking, ed. Sandy Petry (Lubbock: Texas Tech University Press, 1989).

20. Mona Ozouf, *Women's Words: Essay on French Singularity*, trans. Jane Marie Todd (Chicago: University of Chicago Press, 1997), p. 247.

21. *Ibid.*, p. 249.

22. Jean-Jacques Rousseau, *Emile or On Education*, trans. Allan Bloom (New York: Basic Books, 1979), pp. 409, 410.

23. Denis Diderot, *Dialogues* (London: Routledge, 1927), p. 187.

24. Francis Ronsin, *Le Contrat sentimental: Débats sur le mariage, l'amour, le divorce de l'Ancien Régime à la Restauration* (Paris: Auber, 1990), p. 108.

25. Mme de Staël, *Réflexions sur le procès de la reine* (Paris: Mercure de France, 1996), p. 58.

CHAPTER ONE: THE HOSTAGE PRINCESSES

1. *Lettres de la princesse Palatine (1672–1722)* (Paris: Mercure de France, 1985), p. 382

2. One of the German princes of the Holy Roman Empire entitled to elect the Emperor.

3. *Ibid.*, p. 201. As the wife of the king's brother, Madame was her title at the court of Versailles.

4. *Ibid.*, p. 134.

5. *Ibid.*, p. 31

6. *Mémoires de la Margrave de Bayreuth* (Paris: Mercure de France, 1967), p. 62.

7. *Ibid.*, p. 91.

8. *Marie-Antoinette: Correspondance secrète entre Marie-Thérèse et le comte Mercy-Argenteau avec les lettres de Marie-Thérèse et de Marie-Antoinette* (Paris: Librairie Firmin Didot, 1875), vol. 1, p. 3.

9. *Memoirs of Madame Campan on Marie-Antoinette and Her Court* (Boston: J.B. Millet Company, 1909), vol. 1, p. 19.

10. *Lettres de la princesse Palatine*, p. 274.

11. *Ibid.*, pp. 45–46.

12. *Ibid.*, p. 93.

13. As breeders, their conjugal fidelity had to be absolutely above suspicion, while the debauchery of their husbands was taken for granted.

14. *Lettres de la princesse Palatine*, p. 399.

15. *Marie-Antoinette: Correspondance secrète*, vol. 1, p. 75.

16. *Lettres de la princesse Palatine*, p. 65.

17. *Ibid.*, p. 300.

18. *Marie-Antoinette: Correspondance secrète*, vol. 1, p. 24.

19. *Ibid.*, vol. 2, p. 404.

CHAPTER TWO: THE INCORRIGIBLE

1. Prince de Ligne, *Les Plus belles pages du prince de Ligne* (Paris: Mercure de France, 1964), pp. 194–95.

2. Simon Schama, *Citizens: A Chronicle of the French Revolution* (New York: Vintage, 1989), p. 210. See also Sarah Maza's chapter, "The Diamond Necklace Affair Revisited (1785–1786): The Case of the Missing Queen," in *Eroticism and the Body Politic*, ed. Lynn Hunt (Baltimore: Johns Hopkins University Press, 1991). Sarah Maza analyzes with fine precision the narrative and other strategies put to work to turn the queen into the guilty instigator of and main protagonist in an affair in which, in fact, she played no part.

3. *Essais historiques sur la vie de Marie-Antoinette d'Autriche, reine de France, pour servir à l'histoire de cette princesse* (London, 1789), p. 1.

4. *Ibid.*, p. 2.

5. *L'Ancien Moniteur*, no. 20 (January 1791).

6. *Marie-Antoinette: Correspondance secrète entre Marie-Thérèse et le comte Mercy-Argenteau avec les lettres de Marie-Thérèse et de Marie-Antoinette* (Paris: Librairie Firmin Didot, 1875), vol. 2, p. 404.

7. On the new conception of time inaugurated by the Revolution, see my chapter, "L'Héroine du crime: Marie-Antoinette dans les pamphlets," in *La Carmagnole des Muses: L'Homme de lettres et l'artiste dans la Révolution*, ed. Jean-Claude Bonnet (Paris: Armand Colin, 1988).

8. Bull's-Eye, a room at Versailles, named for its circular windows, where the courtesans gathered to discuss the latest news.

9. Edmond and Jules de Goncourt, *Marie-Antoinette* (Paris: Olivier Orban, 1983), p. 147.

10. Robert Darnton, *The Literary Underground of the Old Regime* (Cambridge, MA: Harvard University Press, 1982), pp. 202–203.

11. The miniaturized world that Trianon represented was Marie-Antoinette's chosen mode of escape from the vast panoptical theater created at Versailles by Louis XIV, the Sun King, whose sole presence was supposed to eliminate any shadow in which to hide. As Allen S. Weiss explains, this seizure of power was indissolubly both political and aesthetic: "In his *Mémoires* of 1661, Louis XIV explains to his son, 'Do not be astonished if I so often urge you to work, to see everything, to hear everything.' In the *theatrum mundi* that was to become the court of Versailles, this exhortation — while evoking the omnipotent, omniscient, and omnipresent God with whom the king was identified — actually served the practical purpose of creating the panoptical mechanism of surveillance, which was one of the principal microstructures that guaranteed his power." (quoted in Allen S. Weiss, *Mirrors of Infinity: The French Formal Garden and Seventeenth-Century Metaphysics* [New York: Princeton Architectural Press, 1995], p. 71).

12. Friedrich Nietzsche, *On the Genealogy of Morals*, trans. Walter Kaufmann (New York: Vintage, 1989), p. 37.

13. *Correspondance*, Archives Nationales, 444 AP.

14. *Ibid.*

15. Louis Ferdinand Céline, *Semmelweis et autres écrits médicaux* (Paris: Gallimard, 1977), p. 19.

16. Roberto Calasso, *The Ruin of Kasch*, trans. William Weaver and Stephen Santarelli (Cambridge: Belknap Press, 1994), p. 28.

17. *Mémoires inédits de Mme la comtesse de Genlis* (Paris: Ladvocat, 1825), vol. 1, p. 285.

18. *Vie de Marie-Antoinette d'Autriche, reine de France, femme de Louis XVI, roi des Français [from the loss of her virginity to the first of May 1791, embellished by twenty-six plates, and supplemented by a third section, Paris, at the author's and elsewhere, as Freedom permits]*, pp. 130–32.

19. *Conférence entre Mme de Polignac et Mme de La Motte au parc Saint-James, ou Lettres de M. de Vaudreuil à un abbé fort connu* (London, n. d.), p. 7.

20. *Tel gens tel encens* (n. p., n. d.) pp. 23–24.

21. *Moniteur universel*, November 19, 1793.

22. The final avatar of "His Majesty": when the royal family was at the Tuileries, Marie-Antoinette, at Louis XVI's request, wrote to tell Axel de Fersen to substitute "you" (vous) for "His Majesty" to facilitate their correspondence.

23. *Marie-Antoinette. Correspondance secrète*, vol. 2, p. 1 (July 1773).

24. Louis-Sébastien Mercier, *Le Nouveau Paris*. ed. Jean-Claude Bonnet (Paris: Mercure de France, 1994), p. 50.

25. *Essais historique sur la vie de Marie-Antoinette*, part 2, p. 91.

26. Louis Massignon, *Parole donnée* (Paris: "10/18," 1970) p. 193.

27. Hector Fleischmann, *Les Pamphlets libertins contre Marie-Antoinette* (Geneva: Slatkine, Megariotis Reprints, 1976), p. 100.

28. *Mémoires de Madame Campan, première femme de chambre de Marie-Antoinette* (Paris: Mercure de France, 1988), p. 28.

29. *Marie-Antoinette: Correspondance secrète*, vol. 1, p. 68.

30. *Testament de Marie-Antoinette d'Autriche, ci-devant reine de France* (n. p., 1790), p. 5.

31. *Confession et Repentir de Mme de P[olignac] . . . ou la Nouvelle Madeleine convertie* (n. p., 1789), p. 11.

32. *Description of the Royal Menagerie of Living Animals*, included in this volume; quotation from p. 245.

33. Louis-Sébastien Mercier's motion at the Convention on January 7, 1793 is much milder. The author of *Tableau de Paris* proposed that the royal family be transported to Tahiti or some other island in the south, so that contact with nature, in the simplicity of a fishing hut, would rehabilitate them.

34. *The Testament of Marie-Antoinette, the Widow Capet*, included in this volume; quotation from p. 249.

35. Calasso, *The Ruin of Kasch*, p. 10.

36. Jules Michelet, *Histoire de la Révolution française* (Paris: Laffont, 1979), p. 339.

37. Chateaubriand, *Mémoires d'outre-tombe* (Paris: Gallimard, Bibliothèque de la Pléiade, 1951), vol. 1, p. 709.

38. *Ibid.*, vol. 1, p. 984.

39. Calasso, *The Ruin of Kasch*, p. 4.

40. *Ibid.*, p. 9.

41. *Ibid.*, p. 4.

CHAPTER THREE: QUEEN OF FASHION

1. Chateaubriand, *Mémoires d'outre-tombe* (Paris: Pléiade, 1951), vol. 1, p. 184. The "clipping" is a reference to the guillotine and the "red shirt" refers to the clothing in which the condemned parricides were sent to the guillotine.

2. Marie-Antoinette, in a letter to Mme de Polignac, August 31, 1789; in *Correspondance*, Archives Nationales, 440 AP.

3. Gouverneur Morris, *A Diary of the French Revolution*, vol. 1, ed. Beatrix Cary Davenport (Westport, CT: Greenwood Press, 1972), p. 16.

4. Norbert Elias, *The Court Society*, trans. Edmund Jephcott (Oxford, UK: Basil Blackwell, 1983), p. 103.

5. Gouverneur Morris, *A Diary of the French Revolution*, p. 78.

6. *Lettres de la princesse Palatine (1672–1722)* (Paris: Mercure de France, 1967), p. 163.

7. *Ibid.*, p. 165.

8. *Marie-Antoinette: Correspondance secrète entre Marie-Thérèse et le comte Mercy-Argenteau avec les lettres de Marie-Thérèse et de Marie-Antoinette* (Paris: Librairie Firmin Didot, 1875), vol. 2, p. 64.

9. *Mémoires de Mme Campan, première femme de chambre de Marie-Antoinette* (Paris: Mercure de France, 1988), pp. 87–88.

10. *Ibid.*, p. 88.

11. *Mémoires de la baronne d'Oberkirsch* (Paris: Mercure de France, 1970), p. 302.

12. Simplicity can have serious consequences for a country. In launching a fashion for clothes made of linen, Marie-Antoinette ruined the Lyons silk manufacturers.

13. Edmond and Jules de Goncourt, *La Femme au dix-huitième siècle* (Paris: Flammarion, 1982), p. 257.

14. *Marie-Antoinette: Correspondance secrète*, vol. 2, p. 453.

15. *Ibid.*, p. 307.

16. *Mémoires inédits de Mme la comtesse de Genlis* (Paris: Ladvocat, 1825), vol. 1, pp. 224–25.

17. Jules Michelet, *Histoire de la Révolution française* (Paris: Laffont, 1979), p. 552.

18. *Ibid.*, p. 552.

19. Hector Fleischmann, *Les Pamphlets libertins contre Marie-Antoinette* (Geneva: Slatkine, Megariotis Reprints, 1976), p. 44.

20. *Le Petit Journal du Palais-Royal*, no. 6, p. 12.

21. "Madame ma chère fille, je suis bien aise que mes vieux grisons vous ont voulu faire tant de plaisir." *Marie-Antoinette: Correspondance secrète*, vol. 2, p. 265.

22. *Ibid.*, vol. 2, p. 156.

23. *Le Catéchisme libertin, par Mlle de Théroigne*, ca. 1791, p. 26.

24. *Essais historiques sur la vie de Marie-Antoinette d'Autriche, reine de France, pour servir à l'histoire de cette princesse* (London, 1789), p. 44.

25. Mme Roland, *Mémoires* (Paris: Mercure de France, 1986), pp. 280–81.

26. *Ibid.*, p. 102.

27. *Mémoires inédits de Mme la comtesse de Genlis*, vol. 1, p. 291.

28. L. Prudhomme, [Louise Robert], *Les Crimes des reines de France depuis le commencement de la monarchie jusqu'à Marie-Antoinette* (Paris: Bureau des révolutions de Paris, 1791), Preface, p. 1.

29. Théveneau de Morande, *Anecdotes sur Mme la comtesse du Barry* (London: John Adamsohn, 1776), p. 35.

30. Gérard Walter, ed., *Actes du Tribunal révolutionnaire* (Paris: Mercure de France, 1968), p. 56.

31. *Marie-Antoinette: Correspondance secrète*, vol. 1, p. 370.

32. Mme de Staël, *Réflexions sur le procès de la reine* (Paris: Mercure de France, 1996 [1793]), p. 23.

33. Pierre Saint-Amand, "Adorning Marie-Antoinette," in *Eighteenth Century Life* (November 1991), pp. 30, 32.

Chapter Four: The Female Monster

1. Gérard Walter, ed., *Actes du Tribunal révolutionnaire* (Paris: Mercure de France, 1968), p. 53.

2. Edmond and Jules de Goncourt, *Marie-Antoinette* (Paris: Olivier Orban, 1983), p. 11.

3. Edmond and Jules de Goncourt, *Histoire de la société française pendant la Révolution* (Paris: Charpentier, 1898), p. 236.

4. *Essai historique, ou La Vie de Marie-Antoinette, reine de France et de Navarre, née archiduchesse d'Autriche, le 2 Novembre 1755,* (n. p., 1789), part 2, p. 24.

5. *Essais historiques sur la vie de Marie-Antoinette d'Autriche, reine de France, pour servir à l'histoire de cette princesse* (London, 1789), p. 47.

6. *Oeuvres anonymes du XVIIIe siècle,* Bibliothèque Nationale, Enfer No. 6, (Paris: Fayard, 1987), p. 403.

7. *Essais historiques sur la vie de Marie-Antoinette,* p. 41.

8. *Vie de Marie-Antoinette d'Autriche, reine de France, femme de Louis XVI, roi des Français* (Paris, 1791), p. 5.

9. *Marie-Antoinette: Correspondance secrète entre Marie-Thérèse et le comte Mercy-Argenteau avec les lettres de Marie-Thérèse et de Marie-Antoinette* (Paris: Librairie Firmin Didot, 1875), vol. 3, p. 50.

10. Mme de La Fayette, *The Princesse de Clèves*, trans. Terence Cave (Oxford, UK: Oxford University Press World's Classics, 1992), p. 4.

11. Théveneau de Morande, *Anecdotes sur Mme la comtesse du Barry* (London: John Adamsohn, 1776), p. 151.

12. *Le Portefeuille d'un talon rouge* (n. p., 1780), p. 14. Under Louis XIV's reign red-heeled shoes were fashionable — at the court of Versailles, they were a sign of nobility. In the title of this pamphlet they indicate aristocracy.

13. *Essais historiques sur la vie de Marie-Antoinette,* p. 11.

14. *Ibid.,* p. 72.

15. *Antoinette d'Autriche, ou Dialogues entre Catherine de' Médicis et Frédé-*

gonde reine de France, aux Enfers, pour servir de supplément et de suite à tout ce qui a paru sur la vie de cette princesse (London, 1789), p. 8.

16. *Essais historiques sur la vie de Marie-Antoinette*, p. 63.

17. *Bordel patriotique* (n. p., 1791), p. 36.

18. *The Love Life of Charlie and Toinette* (1779). Reprinted in this volume; quotation from p. 185.

19. Léon Bloy, *La Chevalière de la Mort* (Paris: Mercure de France, 1966), p. 35.

20. Bernard Faÿ, *Louis XVI ou la Fin d'un monde* (Paris: Amiot Dumont, 1955), p. 140.

21. Quoted in Louis de Loménie, *Beaumarchais et son temps* (Paris: Michel Levy, 1856), vol. 1, p. 428.

22. *Le Fouet national*, September 1789.

23. L. Prudhomme [Louise Robert], *Les Crimes des reines de France depuis le commencement de la monarchie jusqu'à Marie-Antoinette* (Paris: Office of the Revolutions of Paris, 1791), pp. 438–39.

24. *Les Bordels de Lesbos, ou le Génie de Sapho* (Saint Petersburg, 1790).

25. *Fureurs utérines de Marie-Antoinette, femme de Louis XVI* (n. p., n. d.), p. 8.

26. *Vie de Marie-Antoinette d'Autriche*, p. 81.

27. *Boudoir de Mme la Duchesse de Polignac et Rapport des scènes les plus curieuses, publiées par un membre de cette académie de lubricité* (n. p., 1790), p. 7.

28. *Ibid.*, p. 7.

29. *Ibid.*, p. 5.

30. *Vie de Marie-Antoinette d'Autriche*, p. 102.

31. Albert Mathiez, *Etudes sur Robespierre (1758–1794)* (Paris: Messidorf & Editions Sociales, 1998), p. 161.

32. On this subject, see Antoine de Baecque's essay, "Pamphlets: Libel and Political Mythology," in *Revolution in Print: The Press in France 1775–1800*, eds. Robert Darnton and Daniel Roche (Berkeley: University of California Press, 1989).

33. Antonomasia is a kind of synecdoche which consists in taking a common noun for a proper noun and a proper noun for a common noun. After

being called "Messalina" and "Isabeau of Bavaria," Marie-Antoinette herself entered the antonomasia process: "But rest assured, in prison you could continue playing your sovereign, your Marie-Antoinette, walking through your rooms at night" (Jean Genet, *The Maids*).

34. La Fontaine, *Fables* (Paris: Gallimard, 1986), p. 94.

35. Gérard Genette, *Figures I* (Paris: Seuil, 1966), p. 9.

36. *Ibid.*, p. 17.

37. *Mémoires justicatifs de la comtesse Valois de La Motte* (London, 1788), p. 19.

38. Louis Massignon, *Parole donnée* (Paris: "10/18," 1970), p. 199.

39. *Mémoires justicatifs de la comtesse Valois de La Motte*, p. 21.

40. *Ibid.*, p. 94.

41. *Désespoir de Marie-Antoinette sur la mort de son frère Léopold II, empereur des Romains, et sur la maladie désespérée de Monsieur, frère du roi de France* (Imprimerie de la Liberté, n.d.), p. 4.

42. *Essais historiques sur la vie de Marie-Antoinette*, p. 102.

43. *Ibid.*, p. 80.

44. *Vie de Marie-Antoinette d'Autriche*, p. 131.

45. *Ibid.*, p. 109.

46. Saint-Just, "Institutions républicaines," in *Oeuvres* (Cité Universelle, 1946), p. 306.

47. *L'Iscariote de la France, ou le Député autrichien* (n. p., October 1789), p. 4.

48. *Vie de Marie-Antoinette d'Autriche*, p. 78.

49. *Ibid.*, p. 123.

CHAPTER FIVE: CHANT OF LOATHING

1. From the expression "à l'école des femmes dangereuses" (in the school of dangerous women), designating the queen and her entourage. See *L'Iscariote de la France, ou le Député autrichien* (n. p., October 1789), p. 12.

2. *Essais historiques sur la vie de Marie-Antoinette d'Autriche, reine de France, pour servir à l'histoire de cette princesse* (London, 1789), p. 3.

3. *Ibid.*, p. 6.

4. Lynn Hunt, "The Many Bodies of Marie-Antoinette: Political Pornography and the Problem of the Feminine in the French Revolution," in ed. Lynn Hunt, *Eroticism and the Body Politic* (Baltimore: Johns Hopkins University Press, 1991), p. 113.

5. *Vie de Marie-Antoinette d'Autriche, reine de France, femme de Louis XVI, roi des Français* (Paris, 1791), p. 69.

6. *Ibid.*, p. 69.

7. *Ibid.*, p. 75.

8. *Ibid.*, p. 77.

9. Antonin Artaud, *Héliogabale ou l'Anarchiste couronné* (Paris: Gallimard, 1979), p. 97.

10. *Antoinette d'Autriche, ou Dialogues entre Catherine de' Médicis et Frédégonde, reine de France, aux Enfers, pour servir de supplément et de suite à tout ce qui a paru sur la vie de cette princesse* (London, 1789), p. 4.

11. *Ibid.*, p. 7.

12. *Ibid.*, p. 12.

13. *Vie de Marie-Antoinette d'Autriche, reine de France, Femme de Louis XVI, roi des Français* (Paris, 1791), p. 7.

14. Camille Desmoulins, *Révolutions de France et de Brabant*, no. 13 (December 12, 1789). The Salic Law (from the body of laws promulgated during the Frankish era, by the Salian Franks) excluded women from direct sucession, and in the later middle ages was extended to exclude women from inheriting the French crown. In 1328, the Salic Law was invoked when there were no direct male heirs in the Capet line, the Valois were then called to the throne. In Schopenhauer's misogynist essay "Of Women" he writes, "There would be no necessity for the Salic Law: it would be a superfluous truism" (*The Works of Schopenhauer*, trans. T. Bailey Sanders [Garden City, NJ: Garden City Publishing, 1928], p. 454).

15. Emile Benveniste, *Problèmes de linguistique générale* (Paris: Gallimard, 1974), p. 255.

16. Gérard Walter, ed., *Actes du Tribunal révolutionnaire* (Paris: Mercure de France, 1968), p. 96.

17. Daniel Arasse, *La Guillotine dans la Révolution*, exhibition catalog for the Musée de la Révolution française (1987), p. 87.

18. The jury had to decide the following questions:

1. Is it established that there were maneuvers and secret dealings with foreign powers and other enemies outside the Republic, said maneuvers and secret dealings tending to provide them with financial assistance, allowing them entry into French territory, and facilitating the progress of their armament?

2. Is Marie-Antoinette of Austria, widow of Louis Capet, convicted of having cooperated in these maneuvers and conducted these secret dealings?

3. Is it established that there was a plot and conspiracy to provoke a civil war within the Republic?

4. Is Marie-Antoinette of Austria, widow of Louis Capet, convicted of having participated in this conspiracy?" (cited in Walter, *Actes du Tribunal révolutionnaire*, pp. 131–32).

A Select Chronology of

Marie-Antoinette's Life

November 2, 1755. Maria-Antonia Josepha Johanna, Archduchess of Austria, is born in Vienna, the daughter of the Empress Maria Theresa of Austria and of Francis I, Duke of Lorraine, Emperor of Germany. Her birth was preceded by those of Joseph (1741), Maria Christina (1742), Maria Elisabeth (1743), Charles Joseph (1745), Maria Amelia (1746), Pierre Leopold (1747), Jeanne-Gabrielle (1750), Maria Joseph (1751), Maria Caroline (1752) and Ferdinand (1754). It was followed by that of Maximilien Franz (1756).

1765. Death of Francis I, to whom little Maria-Antonia was very attached.

1768. The abbé de Vermond becomes Maria-Antonia's preceptor.

May 16, 1770. Marriage of Maria-Antonia, from now on known as Marie-Antoinette, to the Dauphin of France, Louis-Auguste, grandson of Louis XV. This union expressed Maria Theresa's political desire to reinforce the alliance and "diplomatic revolution" of 1756 between France and Austria, until then France's hereditary enemy.

The abbé de Vermond is named Marie-Antoinette's personal advisor. He remained her confidant and was her sole link to childhood.

Beginning of the correspondence between Maria Theresa and Marie-Antoinette.

The comte de Mercy-Argenteau, Austrian Ambassador to France, regularly dispatches secret reports to Maria Theresa on her daughter.

1773. Disgrace and fall of the duc de Choiseul, the major broker in the marriage between Louis-Auguste and Marie-Antoinette.

May 10, 1774. Death of Louis XV. Beginning of Louis XVI's reign. Louis XVI offers Marie-Antoinette the Petit Trianon as a present. The queen's extravagant hairdos and her passion for dress cause a scandal.

Friendship with the princesse de Lamballe, who is named *surintendante* of the Queen's House.

1777. Visit of her elder brother, Emperor Joseph II.

Her friendship with Mme de Polignac begins.

Dec. 20, 1779. A daughter is born and baptized Marie-Thérèse.

1778–1779. War of Succession in Bavaria. Maria Theresa of Austria pressures Marie-Antoinette to influence the king in her favor.

1780. France enters the American War of Independence.

Death of Maria Theresa of Austria.

October 22, 1781. Birth of a son, Louis-Josèphe, heir to the throne. The king's brothers, the comte de Provence and the comte d'Artois, are forced to renounce their dreams of succession.

Mme de Polignac is named Governess of the Children of France. Her family is showered with favors.

1785. Birth of a second son, who receives the title of duc de Normandie.

1785–1786. The Diamond Necklace Affair. The queen is accused of using the cardinal de Rohan to purchase a diamond necklace for which she then refused to pay. On 31 May 1786, the *parlement* declares the cardinal de Rohan innocent and condemns Mme de La Motte, seen as the instigator in the affair, to be branded. In the eyes of the deliriously happy public, the queen is *the* guilty party.

1786. Birth of Sophie-Hélène-Béatrice, who dies at the age of one. The health of the dauphin, Louis-Josèphe, begins to be of grave concern.

May 4, 1789. The meeting of the Estates General gets under way at Versailles.

June 14. Death of Louis-Josèphe.

July 11. The Minister of Finance, Jacques Necker, is dismissed at the height of his popularity.

July 14. The storming of the Bastille.

July 16. Necker is reinstated. The comte d'Artois and most of the courtiers leave Versailles, the Polignac family among them.

October 5–6. A crowd of market women march to Versailles to demand "Bread and the King." The royal family leaves the castle. They are driven to Paris and set up in the Tuileries. Without any consistent policy, the queen wildly forms the most disparate alliances. Her only consistent line: to get help from abroad for the royalists.

June 1791. On June 20, 1791, the royal family surreptitiously left the Tuileries palace in an effort to join counterrevolutionary forces in Germany but were stopped by a pro-revolutionary postman in the town of Varennes near the border and forced to return to Paris.

July 11, 1792. Manifest of the Duke of Brunswick.

August 10. The Parisian crowd storms the Tuileries palace; Louis XVI and Marie-Antoinette are placed under the protection of the National Assembly, and are transferred to the Temple prison.

September 2–6. Massacres in the jails. The princesse de Lamballe is assassinated.

September 22. Abolition of the monarchy. First French Republic is declared.

January 21, 1793. Execution of Louis XVI.

March 10. The Revolutionary Tribunal is created.

July 13. Charlotte Corday assassinates Marat.

August. Marie-Antoinette is separated from her children and locked up in the Conciergerie.

October 14–16. Marie-Antoinette's trial. She is guillotined the morning of October 16.

The Characters

Anne of Austria (1601–1666): daughter of Philip III of Spain and wife to Louis XIII of France, she governed France as regent with the aid of cardinal Mazarin during the minority of Louis XIV (1643–1651).

Artois, comte d': see **Charles X.**

Bailly, Jean-Sylvain (1736–1793): scholar and politician. Bailly was president of the National Assembly in June of 1789, then mayor of Paris following the fall of the Bastille on July 14 of that year. He was guillotined during the Terror for his pro-monarchical stance following Louis XVI's flight to Varennes.

Barnave, Josèphe (1761–1793): a well-known orator during the Constituent Assembly, Barnave was executed during the Terror for his outspoken support of constitutional monarchy.

Beaumarchais, Pierre-Augustin Caron de (1732–1799): inventor, dramatist, diplomat, and arms trader, he was the author of the trilogy *The Barber of Seville*, the controversial *Marriage of Figaro*, and *The Guilty Mother*.

Cagliostro, Joseph Balsamo, comte de (1743–1795): Italian doctor and charlatan. Cagliostro was deeply involved with the occult and the masonic movement. He was popular at the court of Louis XVI, but after compromising himself in the Diamond Necklace Affair, he was exiled from France.

Campan, Jeanne-Louise Genet, Mme (1752–1822): first chambermaid to Marie-Antoinette, and author of a highly sympathetic portrait of the queen in her published memoirs.

Charles X (1757–1836): brother of Louis XVI, he emigrated from France in 1789 in order to organize the Counter-Revolution. He succeeded to the throne in 1824, but his reactionary policies led to the Revolution of 1830 and the "July Monarchy" of Louis-Philippe d'Orleans.

Choiseul, Etienne-François, duc de (1719–1785): foreign minister under Louis XV from 1758 to 1770, he was the man primarily responsible for arranging the marriage of Marie-Antoinette and Louis XVI that capped the "diplomatic revolution," reversing centuries of Franco-Austrian political rivalry.

Corday, Charlotte (1768–1793): a sympathizer with the Girondin faction of the National Convention, Charlotte Corday assassinated the Montagnard journalist Jean-Paul Marat in his bath tub on July 13, 1793. She was guillotined four days later. She declared at her trial, "I was a republican well before the Revolution, and have never lacked energy."

Danton, Georges-Jacques (1759–1794): a prominent Montagnard, organizer of national defense and the revolutionary tribunals during the Convention, Danton was one of the original members of the executive Committee of Public Safety, but was eventually purged by his rival Robespierre, who had him executed in April 1794.

Desmoulins, Camille (1760–1794): lawyer and journalist. Desmoulins founded *Les Révolutions de France et de Brabant*, a highly successful journal which ran from 1789 to 1791. A member of the Convention, he advocated a policy of clemency in his second journal, *Le Vieux cordelier* (1793), and was executed alongside Danton in April 1794.

Du Barry, Jeanne Bécu, comtesse (1743–1793): last mistress and favorite of Louis XV, she was guillotined during the Terror in 1793.

Eon, Charles de Beaumont d' (1728–1810): political agent for Louis XV, he gained notoriety for his transvestitism.

Fersen, Axel, Count of (1755–1810): an illustrious Swedish nobleman, he was a courtier, soldier and politician. He met Marie-Antoinette in 1778 and they soon became intimate friends (according to some, lovers). Fersen was a staunch advocate of divine-right monarchy, a stance for which he was assassinated by a mob in Stockholm.

Feuillants: a faction of constitutional monarchists who broke away from the Jacobin club after the king's failed attempt to flee France in the summer of 1791 (cf. "Flight to Varennes"). Although they had more deputies in the Legislative Assembly (1791–1792) than did the republican inclined Girondins, they were unable to prevent the fall of the monarchy on August 10, 1792, an event which politically discredited them.

Francis I, duc de Lorraine (1708–1765): father of Marie-Antoinette, he married Maria Theresa in 1736 and became Holy Roman Emperor in 1745.

Fredegonde (ca. 545–597): wife of the Frankish king Chilperic I, she was notorious for having stopped at no crime to attain the throne.

Genlis, Stéphanie-Félicité, comtesse de Brussard (1746–1830): tutor of the children of Philippe-Égalité, duc d'Orleans. She wrote several works on education, a book on etiquette, and her memoires.

Gorsas, Antoine Josèphe (1752–1793): was a member of the Convention, journalist, and founder of the *Courrier de Versailles à Paris*, which he continued under the title of *Courrier des 83 départements*. He was guillotined in 1793 as a Girondin.

Gouges, Olympe de (1748–1793): playwright, woman of letters, and feminist, author of *A Declaration of the Rights of Woman* in 1791. She was imprisoned for penning a pamphlet attacking Robespierre and sentenced to death.

Gravier, Charles, comte de Vergennes (1717–1787): became the minister of foreign affairs in 1774, when Louis XVI came to the thrown. The king had great confidence in him, and he was named head of the board of finance in 1783.

Hébert, Jacques-René (1757–1794): radical politician and journalist, he was the author of *Le Père Duchesne*, one of the most violent, popular, and scabrously written journals of the French Revolution. He was an outspoken apologist for the use of political terror, having applauded the September Massacres of 1792. He was condemned and guillotined by Robespierre and the Committee of Public Safety, who feared him as a political rival.

Hébertist: political follower of the revolutionary journalist Jacques-René Hébert. The Hébertists were populist and violent in outlook, tending to view the French Revolution as a battle between the rich and the poor. Their demands for fixed pricing on bread set them at odds with the economic liberals in the Convention.

Joseph II (1741–1790): brother of Marie-Antoinette, Holy Roman Emperor and ruler of Austria from 1765 to 1790, Joseph II was the model of an "enlightened despot."

Kéralio-Robert, Louise de (1758–1822): born into an old Breton family of the enlightened liberal aristocracy, she was a prolific novelist and historian, publishing works of feminist criticism before 1789 (*Adélaide*; *History of Elisabeth, Queen of England*, and the twelve-volume *Collection of the Best Works Composed by Women*); during the revolutionary period (*Crimes of the Queens of France*), and during the Restoration (*Amélia and Caroline*).

Lafayette, Marie-Josèphe du Motier, marquis de (1757–1834): French general and politician, he played a prominent role as a Franco-American liaison during the American War for Independence. A liberal royalist, he was made head of the National Guard in 1789, but fled France with the fall of the monarchy in 1792. He returned to France under the amnesty of Napoleon. Lafayette served several terms in the Chamber of Deputies during the restoration and played a prominent role in the Revolution of 1830.

La Fayette, Marie-Madeleine, Mme de (1634–1693): French woman of letters. She is the author of several novels, most notably *The Princess of Clèves*, as well as her memoires.

La Motte, Jeanne, comtesse de (1756–1791): a court intriguer, she was compromised during the Diamond Necklace Affair and forced to flee to England.

Lamballe, Marie-Thérèse-Louise de (1749–1792): French noblewoman and intimate friend of Marie-Antoinette. She was imprisoned in 1792, refused to subscribe to the oath against the monarchy and was torn to pieces by the mob.

Louis XIV (1638–1715): king of France from 1643 to 1715. His absolutist vision of the French monarchy's grandeur was epitomized by the château de Versailles. The endemic wars of his reign brought France some territorial gains, but they severely damaged the domestic economy, and he died amid harsh criticism.

Louis XV (1710–1774): great-grandson of Louis XIV, he ruled as king of France from 1715 to 1774. Louis XV was unable to maintain the charismatic style of leadership upon which his great-grandfather had established an absolute monarchy. His reign witnessed France's diplomatic realignment with Austria in 1756 under the influence of Choiseul and Mme de Pompadour.

Louis XVI (1754–1793): very religious, he was wed to Marie-Antoinette in 1770 and ascended to the throne of France in 1774. His refusal to definitively support or resist the French Revolution led to his unpopularity with revolutionaries and counter-revolutionaries alike. Tainted by the "flight to Varennes" in June 1792, his monarchical rule was suspended after a Parisian crowd stormed the Tuileries palace on August 10, 1792. Compromising documents revealed his counterrevolutionary collusion with Austria. He was condemned for treason and guillotined.

Louis XVIII (1755–1824): younger brother of Louis XVI, he carried the title of comte de Provence. His ambition and jealousy led him to participate in the libellous attacks on the person of Louis XVI. In exile during the Revolution, in 1795 (upon the purported death of his nephew, Louis Joseph XVII), he proclaimed himself king of France. Louis XVIII only returned to assume the crown in 1814, when the Bourbon monarchy was restored followed the defeat of Napoleon. He reigned until his death in 1824.

Louis of France (1785–?): second son of Louis XVI and Marie-Antoinette, he disappeared in 1795, and was rumored to have died in prison.

Louis-Philippe I (1773–1850): son of Philippe d'Orléans, [Philippe-Égalité], he reigned as king of France from 1830 to 1848, during the "July Monarchy." He was known for his liberal-bourgeois policies, but domestic discontent brought him down from power in the Revolution of 1848. He finished his life in exile in England.

Ludwig II of Bavaria (1845–1886): was purported to be a mad king who ruled Bavaria from 1864 to 1886. Friend and patron of Richard Wagner, he is famous for his extravagant, baroque building projects, such as Schloss Neuschwanstein and Schloss Herrenschiemsee. He adored Marie-Antoinette. He drowned in lake Starnberg under mysterious circumstances.

Madame: at the court of Versailles, a generic term used to denote a sister or sister-in-law of the king of France.

Maintenon, Françoise D'Aubigné, marquise de, (1635–1719): mistress of Louis XIV, who married her in a secret ceremony in 1684 after the death of his first wife. She had a great deal of influence over the king and is said to have encouraged him to revoke the Edict of Nantes in 1685, suspending the privileges of Protestants in France.

Marat, Jean-Paul (1743–1793): physician and Montagnard journalist, founder of *L'Ami du peuple,* he was an instigator of the September Massacres of 1792 and the arrest of the Girondins in 1793. He was stabbed to death in his bathtub by Charlotte Corday.

Maria Theresa (1717–1780): wife of Francis I, duc de Lorraine and mother of Marie-Antoinette, she ruled over the Austro-Hungarian Empire from 1740 to 1765, at which point she administered with her son, Joseph II, until her death. She was, however, responsible for a number of fiscal, administrative and educational reforms, despite opposing the progressive ideas of the Encylopedists.

Marie Leszczynska (1703–1768): daughter of the Polish king Stanislas Leszczinski, she was the wife of Louis XV, by whom she had ten children.

Marie-Thérèse (1638–1683): daughter of Philip IV of Spain, she was married to Louis XIV in 1660.

Medici, Catherine de (1519–1589): wife of Henry II and regent during the minorities of François II and Charles IX, she attempted to balance Protestant and Catholic factions during the French Wars of Religion. She was known for her political pragmatism and lack of scruple, and many blamed her for the massacre of thousands of French Protestants on St. Bartholemew's Day in 1572.

Mercier, Louis-Sébastien (1740–1814): French journalist and dramatist whose multi-volume *Tableau de Paris* offers a vivid panorama of Parisian life in the eighteenth century.

Mercy-Argenteau, Florimund, comte de (1727–1794): Austrian ambassador to France from 1766 to 1790, he helped arrange the marriage of Louis XVI and Marie-Antoinette. He remained a confidante of the queen even after his transfer to England in 1790.

Méricourt, Théroigne de (1762–1817): having led the life of a singer and adventuress, the woman they called "the Beauty of Liège" or "the Beautiful Foreigner" became passionate about the Revolution. She was a fiery orator and favored the Girondins. One day, passing by the Tuileries, she imprudently provoked a group of Jacobins. They gave her a public whipping that sent her mad; Théroigne was locked up at the Salpêtrière.

Mirabeau, Gabriel Honoré, comte de (1715–1791): the most prominent orator of the early phase of the French Revolution. Although a noble, his profligacy and liberal views made him unpopular with the aristocracy, and he was elected to the Estates General by the Third Estate. By 1791, shortly before his death, he had made a pact with Louis XVI to serve as his advisor.

Monsieur: at the court of Versailles, a generic term referring to the brother of the king of France.

Montagnard: the most radical faction on the left during the Convention. After their triumph over the Girondins, by the spring of 1794 the Montagnards were able to organize a more united political front, using the Committee of Public Safety to organize the war effort against the allied powers of Europe. The faction's leaders included Robespierre, Marat, Danton, and Saint-Just.

Napoleon I (1769–1821): born in Corsica, made a general during the wars of the French Revolution, his coup d'état in 1799 paved the way for his rule as emperor of France from 1804 until his defeat at Waterloo in 1815.

Palatine, Elisabeth Charlotte of Bavaria, princesse (1652–1722): second wife of the duc d'Orléans (1640–1701), the brother of Louis XIV. Her brutally frank correspondance documents the moral history of her brother-in-law's reign.

Philippe d'Orléans (1674–1723): son of the princesse Palatine (Elisabeth Charlotte of Bavaria), he became regent of France upon the death of Louis XIV in 1715. His rule was characterized by a reaction against many of Louis's absolutist policies, but it was marred by the failure of the government finance system organized by John Law (1671–1729).

Polignac, Yolande-Martine Gabrielle, duchesse Jules de (1749–1793): she was an intimate friend of Marie-Antoinette.

Pompadour, Antoinette Poisson, marquise de (1721–1764): favorite of Louis XV, she was a strong advocate of France's alliance with Austria during the Seven Years War (1756–1763), and a great patron of arts and letters.

Provence, comte de: see Louis XVIII.

Rais, Gilles de (1396–1440): Marshall of France during the Hundred Years War (1346–1454), he helped Joan of Arc lift the English siege of Orleans in 1429. His murderous lust led him to torture children to death in his castle for pleasure. He was eventually sentenced to death for this after a trial during which he admitted his crimes and expressed repentance.

Robespierre, Maximillian de (1758–1794): lawyer, deputy to the National Assembly and the Convention. The soul of the Committee of Public Safety, he made a political principle out of the use of terror to defend republican virtue. After eliminating his rivals Danton and Hébert in the spring of 1794, he in turn fell from power and was guillotined the following July, ending the Terror and beginning the so-called "Thermidorean Reaction."

Rohan, Edouard, prince de (1734–1803): cardinal and grand chaplain of France, ambassador to Vienna, he was disgraced during the Diamond Necklace Affair.

Roland de la Platrière, Mme (1754–1793): a great reader of Rousseau, she was remarkably intelligent and studious. She married Roland de la Platrière in 1780 and collaborated with him on *L'Encyclopédie méthodique*. She moved from Lyon to Paris, where she was drawn by the Revolution. There she met the Girondins, Brissot, Pétion, Buzot, with whom she was already in correspondence. She held a salon and was enthusiastic about the beginnings of the Revolution. In 1792, Roland was named minister of the interior. Arrested under the Terror, she wrote her admirable *Mémoires* in prison. She died at the guillotine.

Sade, Donatien Alphonse François, marquis de (1740–1814): notorious libertine and scandalous writer. He spent most of his adult life in prison. His best known works are *Justine*, *Juliette*, *One Hundred and Twenty Days of Sodom* and *Philosophy in the Bedroom*.

Saint-Just, Louis de (1767–1794): right hand man of Robespierre on the Committee of Public Safety, he successfully organized the army of the Rhine during the campaign of 1793. He was guillotined with Robespierre in June of 1794.

Saint-Simon, Louis de Rouvroy, duc de (1675–1755): member of a high-ranking noble family, he was the author of a celebrated series of memoirs which penetratingly characterize daily life at the court of Versailles between 1694 and 1723.

Sévigné, Marie de Rabutin-Chantal, marquise de (1626–1696): woman of letters and wit. She is best known for the correspondence she kept with her daughter for twenty-five years. It was published as a model of the epistolary genre and a literary masterpiece.

Staël, Mme de (1766–1817): daughter of Jacques Necker (1732–1804), she was one of France's foremost romantic novelists. Her books include *Delphine, Corinne,* and *On Germany.* Her liberal tendencies made her unpopular with Napoleon.

Talleyrand-Périgord, Charles Maurice de, prince de Bénévent (1754–1838): bishop of Autun during the ancien régime, he became president of the National Assembly in 1790, then foreign minister during the Directory and under Napoleon. He cast off his allegiance with the latter in time to represent France at the Congress of Vienna (1815), which permitted him to continue in a political capacity during the restoration.

Vergennes, Charles Gravier, comte de (1717–1787): named minister for foreign affairs under Louis XVI in 1774, he became head of the council of finance in 1783.

The Pamphlets

LES
AMOURS
DE
CHARLOT ET TOINETTE

Piece dérobée A V.......

Scilicet is superis labor est, ea cura quietos
sollicitat.......

Virg. Æneid.

MDCCLXXIX

The Love Life

of Charlie and Toinette

A Play Stolen from V——[1]

Scilicet is superis labor est, ea cura quietas sollicitat . . .
— Virgil, *The Aeneid*

1779

A young and frisky Queen,
Whose most August Spouse was a bad fuck,
From time to time, most prudently,
    Relieved herself of her misery,
By putting into play whatever
A Mind tired of waiting and a badly fucked Cunt could devise.
    In sweet reverie,
Her pretty little Body hunched, naked, stark naked,
Sometimes, at night, on the down of a soft wing chair,
She unburdened herself of the day's restraints
With the help of a certain finger, Love's Porter,
And burned her Incense to the God of Cythera;
Sometimes, dying of boredom in the middle of a lovely day,
She writhed all alone in her bed:
Her throbbing tits, her lovely eyes, and her mouth,
Half parted, softly panting,

Seemed to invite the challenge of a good fuck.
    In these Lustful positions,
Antoinette would rather not have
Remained at foreplay,
And that L——[2] had fucked her better;
But what can one say?
           It is well known that that poor Gent,
      Condemned three or four times
      By the salubrious Faculty [of Medicine],
      For total impotence,
      Cannot satisfy Antoinette.
      Thoroughly convicted of this calamity,
      Since his matchstick
      Is about as thick as a bit of straw,
      And always limp and curled up,
      His Cock's only good for his pocket;
      Instead of fucking, he is fucked
      Like the Bishop of Antioch.
D'A——,[3] feeling the sap rising triumphantly one day,
And the desire to fuck rekindling,
Threw himself at the Queen's feet, trembling with hope;
His voice keeps failing him as he tries to speak,
He squeezes and strokes her beautiful hands and
Lets his impatient flame flicker;
He shows he's a little troubled, troubling her in turn;
Winning over Toinette only took a day in fact:
Princes and Kings get down to Love very swiftly.
    In a fine alcove artfully gilded,
Not too dark and not too light,
On a soft sofa, covered in velvet,
The August beauty bestows her charms;
The Prince presents the Goddess his cock:

Delicious moment of fucking and tenderness!

Her Heart is beating, love and modesty

Paint the Beauty with a gorgeous blush;

But modesty passes, and Love alone remains:

The Queen feebly defends herself, she weeps.

The eyes of the proud d'A ——, dazzled, enraptured,

Lit up with a burning flame, run over her beautiful features:

Ah, who indeed could help but worship them!

Below a finely turned neck, which puts alabaster to shame,

Sit two pretty tits, nicely molded, separate,

That gently throb, swollen with Love:

A little Rose stands up on them both.

Tit, O charming Tit, who never sits still,

You seem to invite one's hand to squeeze you,

One's eyes to contemplate you, one's mouth to kiss you.

Antoinette is divine, everything about her is ravishing:

The sweet surrender to which she succumbs,

Seems to lend her greater grace:

Pleasure embellishes her; Love is a great cosmetic.

D'A —— knows her by heart and kisses her all over;

His member is a firebrand, his heart a furnace.

He kisses her lovely arms, her pretty little Cunt,

Here a buttock, there a tit.

He gently slaps her bouncing bum,

Thigh, belly, belly button, the center of all things nice;

The Prince kisses her everywhere in his sweet madness;

And without realizing he looks like a Dolt,

Carried away as he is by his extreme ardor,

He would like to shoot straight at Love's bull's-eye.

Feigning to avoid what she craves, Antoinette

Only half gives in, dreading the shock:

D'A —— seizes the moment, and vanquished Toinette

Feels at last how sweet it is to be well and truly fucked.
    While love tenderly enfolds them
And Charles, holding her, makes her beg for mercy,
Antoinette quivers, already in her eyes
    The pleasures of the Gods are revealed:
They are close to bliss, but fate is a traitor:
The Bell rings...a diligent page,
Too keen to obey, disturbs them by barging in...
To open and introduce himself...see all and disappear
        Took only a second.
        Stunned by his disgrace,
        D'A —— quit his place.
        The Beauty groaned,
        Looked down and blushed,
        Without so much as a word:
The Prince consoles her with a fresh kiss:
"Forget, dear Queen, forget this mishap,
        If this overeager importunate
        Has postponed our joy,
        Misfortune suffered often
        Gives pleasure sharper bite.
"So," said the Handsome d'A ——, "let's make up for lost time."
        En route he tried
        A bolder stroke
        Which the Queen resisted
        With a show of force,
Making their Amorous transports even more piquant,
And displaying Love's hidden treasures all the more.
Dear Reader, our lovers fucked each other so hard
    That their slapping bums gave them away.
Up bobs "Giles" for the second time:
"Your Majesty rang?..." "For God's sake! This is deliberate,"

The Royal Dildo

Publisher's Note

Tired from my patrolling and sentry duty, and finding myself outside the Tuileries at three in the morning, with not a living soul in sight, I was gripped by fear, and hid as well as I could in my tiny sentinel's box. Sleep came and calmed me; but not for long. I clearly heard a voice say to me, "Why are you wearing clothes your lack of courage doesn't entitle you to have, instead of staying in your shop to feed your wife and children? Take this manuscript, go and print it and distribute it in all the towns, and remember that if, within twenty-four hours, the public isn't informed of the facts contained in this little book and you are still wearing that uniform, you will be hanged." The fear that had sent me off to sleep now made me fall flat on my face. I called for help; no one came. As it was pouring rain, I got up and went to seek shelter. Imagine my surprise to find the manuscript that I am now passing on to you as fast as I can, for fear of being hanged! I urge you, my dear citizens, to abandon your uniforms, if you have no more courage than I do. If you dispute the validity of this manuscript, I cannot offer proof; you know how I came by it — I wash my hands of it.

AMEN

LE
GODMICHÉ
ROYAL

1789.

The Royal Dildo

1789

Conversation Between Juno and Hebe[1]

JUNO
(alone, with her skirts hitched up,
playing with her mound of Venus)

Admirable part of a much scorned cunt,
Obliging support for frizzy black hair,
Muff once charming in the eyes of my betrayer,
Alas! Bear the brunt of my latest injury:
The bastard carts elsewhere the incense that is my due;
His cock is limp for me and stiffens for some arsehole.
O Rage! Despair! My poor little pussy,
Jupiter's[2] member no longer cherishes you,
However agreeably placed you are below my navel.
Your only hope is an inanimate tool.
        (She takes a dildo from her workbag.)
Feeble but beneficial semblance of a cock,
Happy invention that we owe to the monastery,
Naturally you please my inflamed cunt:
You're even better than the end of my finger.
        (She starts masturbating.)
Wait a minute! While Jupiter's buggering Ganymede,
Fancy Juno's being reduced to this sad remedy!
Good God! While my husband's treacherous balls,

Of which I'm so often starved, shoot their broth
Into secret places that make Nature blush,
Am I to be satisfied with a simple replica!
No; you'll sooner see a repentant Carmelite friar
Go off and preach in a convent, his cock between his legs.
It's about time I finally avenged this outrage:
If it's true that any arsehole can lure Jupiter,
From now on any cock can fuck Juno;
I'll put my illustrious cunt to good use.
Hebe, dear; show yourself!

* * *

HEBE

At your service,
Mighty Queen; sorry I'm in my nightie
But Hercules was fucking me in your antechamber, Madame,
To keep me busy while I was waiting.

JUNO
(softly)

She spends her life screwing anything that moves;
What a happy fate! How I envy her!
Ah! If only I had some good fuck's cock right now!
I'd fuck my head off with him on the spot!

HEBE

What does that look mean, this deathly silence?
What am I to make of these mournful sighs?

194

If I may say what I think, Madame,
You fuck with the best of them —
So why the daggers? Has some fucking ghoul
Finally given you the clap?
Your cunt wasn't made for such an affront;
Let's see that poker.

JUNO

Here.

HEBE

What the ... !

JUNO

(laughing)
It's a dildo.

HEBE

Ye Gods! What an instrument! Well, I'm delighted
To see you're keeping yourself amused till better things come
along.

*(They sing a duet to the tune of "Your heart,
lovely shepherdess.")*

In nature everything fits in somewhere,
Fish fuck in the sea,
Goats couple on the plain

And midges in the air:
Let's fuck, let's fuck till we're out of breath,
All cocks are made for cunts.

JUNO

Indeed, I could do with savoring
The pleasure a nice long cock can give!
The dried-out lips of my burning cunt
Fold sadly over my vagina.
Heavens! I really need some good fuck's cock
To come and water them, and restore their vigor.
Like a rose, in the middle of a garden bed, which
Half opens, closes, then falls to the ground,
Or, like an oyster away from the sea, in shifting sands,
Yawning at the first breeze.

HEBE

What a thing to say! It stirs my soul;
You mean you reign, Madame, but you don't get fucked!
I spurn the throne and all its empty honors;
A single cock is worth a scepter: the devil take privileges
And all that fate blindly offers us.
A pair of balls are worth more than the most illustrious crown.

JUNO

Ah, my dear Hebe, I couldn't agree more!
But one owes something to one's rank, you know.
You know that a princess, doomed to unhappiness,
Can't chose to marry as she'd like;

But your advice is welcome; how it flatters my heart!
Where there's a will, there's a way: let's do some hard fucking.

HEBE

At last you've come around, as I'd hoped you would.
Say but the word, Madame, and you'll be fucked.
You could instantly form twenty battalions
Of thirty thousand cocks armed with lovely balls,
And give your illustrious cunt free rein;
Just say the word and I'll send them over:
Priapus with his square cock, Pan with the cock of Triton,
Silenus with his piercing cock, more lively than a fish,
And a thousand other rods all in a row
Will fuck your royal snatch till it's dripping.
Oh, Madame: how lovely to content your cunt
With the strokes of such vigorous cocks!
Add your own strokes while you're at it,
And satisfy, if you can, your desire to fuck.
But if, through some unforeseen mishap,
You get tired of being shafted,
I'll exercise an actress's rights,
And lead you off into the wings.

JUNO

Go, fly, dear Hebe, round up your pals,
Encircle my cunt with a battalion of cocks;
You'll see how I excel in fucking.
Choose well, Hebe, prove your zeal to me;
Don't let your senses be deceived by appearances:
A beautiful exterior often hides a rotten inside.

197

Don't bring me, for instance, those fucking pricks
Who're rooted to the spot with ecstasy at the sight of a cunt,
And are scarcely capable, even at the peak of their desire,
Of gently brushing the center of pleasure,
And so amuse themselves, so to speak, with fiddling.
Take care you don't bring back that pack of turds,
Mooning pimps, fake marquis,
Who spend half their time gazing at their reflections,
Those splendid specimens they call fops;
At the signal to advance, they turn traitor:
Their cocks at first seem hale and hearty,
But the bugger shoots his load in a second and scurries off!
I don't want any pale poets either,
Interpreters of the language of the blazing skies,
All too familiar with the game of five-to-one;
When they see a cunt, their importunate sword,
Immediately coming to the aid of their fantastic verve,
Gives them, despite themselves, the jesuitical unction.
Nor do I want any of those puffed up cocks,
Superbly swollen, but not with desire or pleasure:
In vain they agitate their priapic lumps,
They haven't got lust or a fuck in their balls.
To get to the point and make myself clear:
You might as well put poison in your cunt.
Dear Hebe, that's not what's needed
To calm Juno's burning cunt.
I want cocks whose solid shaft
Knows neither rest nor measure in fucking;
Entertaining cocks whose ticklish knob
Knows how to hose my amorous fibers at a stroke:
Cocks, in short, which, proud of a surprise attack,
Force me immediately to parry.

HEBE

Leave it to me, I know how each one fucks.
Madame, your tastes will be catered for;
I hereby declare that, whatever my desire,
I'll never masturbate or fuck again
If the least of the cocks I have in mind
Doesn't get you off twenty times, no exaggeration.

JUNO

That's promising a lot.

HEBE

The smallest of the cocks of these gay dogs
Is at least fifteen inches long.

JUNO

That's how I like them. And the circumference?

HEBE

The smallest is eight inches, by the looks of it.

JUNO
(dreaming)

Fifteen inches long and eight around!
Ah! my cunt's creaming just thinking about it.
Bring them on, let them flood my cunt!

Hebe, go and tell them that sweet Juno,
Since you'll have to name me, is hotter than embers;
That I'm dissatisfied and free with my favors!
But are they really all robust fucks —
Hebe, can I believe you? Forgive my anxiety,
But what if their cocks aren't built to last,
And, on entering my cunt, however vast and wide,
Pull out straight away? . . . No, no, you know your stuff,
Your amorous flame has never let me down;
Let them come, it's as good as done, I'll fuck my head off,
I'll plant horns and more horns on my husband's head;
It's the sorry wimp's turn to find out today
What revenge both rage and love can inspire.
Let them instantly appear, my fanny's well washed,
My petticoat and skirts are hitched high;
The love juices running from my cunt by the bucketful
Will be thought by mortals to be the second Flood.
                    (Exit Hebe)

JUNO
(alone)

Futile fears engendered by ignorance,
Fed by weakness and maintained by imprudence!
Too scrupulous remorse!
Don't come and spoil the ardor of my passion
When I'm in the throes of sweet pleasure,
Or spread your deadly poison over fate.
My cunt speaks; that's enough, what does the rest matter?
This lascivious twitching in my randy cunt,
This is my sole oracle; it must be heeded.
Fuck virtue, that's merely a chimera;

A really amorous cunt can fuck its own father:
Delectable children, bring Juno off;
Voluptuous tools, whether cock or cunt,
You who know so well the titillating custom
Of bursting a maidenhead in the twinkling of an eye:
Pleasures, sons of Venus, leave your abode;
Come and preside over my court for my pleasure.

*(A troupe of Pleasures of different sexes, naked,
enter the stage and perform an erotic dance.)*

Seeing these leaping cocks and dancing pussies,
Whose nascent down covers their burgeoning flowers,
I feel in my cunt the sweet fury
Of pleasure heat me up and fuck me to the core.

(Bibliothèque Nationale, Enfer 665, Enfer 665 bis;
Bibliothèque Historique de la Ville de Paris, 967980)

NOTES

1. *Juno*: wife of Jupiter and queen of the gods. *Hebe*: the goddess of youth, in charge of pouring nectar at Jupiter's table. In this text, Juno designates Marie-Antoinette, Hebe either Mme de Lamballe or Mme de Polignac.

2. Jupiter designates Louis XVI.

L'AUTRICHIENNE

EN

GOGUETTES,

OU

L'ORGIE ROYALE.

Opéra Proverbe.

Veni, vidi.

Composé par un garde du corps et publié depuis la liberté de la Presse, et mis en musique par la Reine. (1)

(1) La Reine, élève de feu Sacchini, et protectrice de tout ce qui est compositeur ultramontain, a la ferme persuasion qu'elle est bonne musicienne, parce qu'elle estropie quelques sonates sur son clavessin, et qu'elle chante faux dans les concerts qu'elle donne in petto et où elle a soin de ne laisser entrer que de vils adulateurs. Quant à Louis xvi, on peut se faire une idée de son goût pour l'harmonie en apprenant que les sons discordans et insupportables de deux flambeaux d'argent frottés avec force sur une table de marbre ont des attraits pour son oreille anti-musicale.

1789.

The Austrian Woman on the RAMPAGE, or the Royal Orgy

an operatic proverb

Veni, vidi

Composed by a Royal Bodyguard,
published since the Freedom of the Press,
*and set to music by the Queen**

1789

Dramatis Personae:

Louis XVI
The Queen
The Comte d'Artois
The Duchesse de Polignac
Royal Bodyguards

---

* The Queen, a pupil of the late Sacchini, and protectress of all foreign composers, is of the firm persuasion that she is a fine musician because she can murder a few sonatas on her harpsichord and sing flat at her secret concerts, where she is careful to admit vile sycophants only. As for Louis XVI, one can get an idea of his taste for harmony when one learns that the discordant and unbearable noise of two silver candlesticks rubbed hard on a marble table sounds sweet to his antimusical ear.

The scene takes place in the Queen's apartments.

SCENE I

BODYGUARDS' CHORUS
(drinking)

Let's vary our pleasures,
Between Bacchus and the God of the Cask.
The example they set us here
Inflames our desires.

A GUARD

To arms! Here comes Her Majesty.

ANOTHER GUARD

There'll be an orgy tonight, the female Ganymede is with the
Queen.

ANOTHER GUARD

And the beloved d'Artois is caught between vice and virtue.
Guess who vice is.

A GUARD

There's no need to guess; all I can see is that god's ubiquity.

SCENE II
The Comte d'Artois, the Queen, Mme de Polignac

THE QUEEN

*(to Mme de Polignac, who
steps aside to let her pass)*

Come, come, my sweet.

THE COMTE D'ARTOIS
*(gently pushing the Queen
from behind, grabbing hold of her buttocks)*

In you go as well. *(In the Queen's ear:)* Oh! What a bum! It's so firm and bouncy!

THE QUEEN
(whispering to the Comte d'Artois)

If my heart were as firm, would we be so good together?

THE COMTE D'ARTOIS

Quiet, you little fool, or I'll give my brother another son tonight.

THE QUEEN

Oh no! Let's gather pleasure's blooms, but make sure we leave the fruit this time.

THE COMTE D'ARTOIS

All right, I'll try to be careful.

THE QUEEN

Let's be seated.

MME DE POLIGNAC

But where's the King?

THE QUEEN

What are you worried about? He'll be along to bore us soon enough.

Trio: the Queen, the Comte d'Artois, Mme de Polignac

THE QUEEN

When I see before me
Pleasure, Love, and the Graces;
Set me in their footsteps,
It is to follow the law of joy.

THE COMTE D'ARTOIS
(to the Queen)

Oh what bliss to be near the one I love;
My heart's overwhelmed with pleasure,
I have no other desire.

MME DE POLIGNAC

Adorable Princess,
what joy for me,
when I can at any moment
plunge your senses
into the sweetest intoxication!

Together
When I see before me
Pleasure, Love, and the Graces;
Set me in their footsteps,
It is to follow the law of joy.

MME DE POLIGNAC

Here comes the King.

SCENE III

The same. Louis XVI

THE QUEEN
(*simpering*)

You take your time! What kept you?

LOUIS

I was busy finishing a lock, which I'm very happy with.

THE QUEEN

You must be tired! Have a nice big glass of bubbly champagne.

LOUIS

Don't mind if I do. *(He drinks)*

THE QUEEN

How about another?

LOUIS

No. I want to stay sober tonight; I must be in council early in the morning. When one's senses are dull, the mind loses its ability to judge properly.

THE QUEEN

All you're required to do is sit. Your council will do what it always does: whatever it likes.

LOUIS

It's true there's no point in wanting to do the right thing; those gentlemen always manage to get me to do something stupid.

THE QUEEN

Still, that's good enough for *the frogs of the Seine.**

Quartet

THE QUEEN

Let's laugh, let's revel,
Make use of our power;
Squander all the money
Of our good Parisians.

Together

Let's laugh, let's revel,
Make use of our power;
Squander all the money
Of our good Parisians.

The King, who has emptied one bottle and three-fourths of the next, falls asleep with his head on the table.

MME DE POLIGNAC

The Guards have retired, the King is asleep.

THE COMTE D'ARTOIS

That's what I call an obliging brother, and a drunken scepter.

* Familiar expression of the Queen's to designate the inhabitants of Paris.

THE QUEEN

Let him have his fill and let's make the most of it.

THE COMTE D'ARTOIS
(kissing the Queen on the mouth)
Well said.

All three get up from the table. The Queen goes and sits on a couch.

THE QUEEN
(stretching out)

Oh, how nice it is here!

THE COMTE D'ARTOIS
(sliding his hand under the Queen's skirt and settling his middle finger on the royal privates)

Ah! It's even nicer here!

THE QUEEN
(to the Comte d'Artois, who starts to move his finger faster and faster)

Ooh, ah! ... Stop it, d'Artois, you're making me come.

MME DE POLIGNAC

So, Monsieur le Comte, you're usurping my rights?
That's not very nice! I don't usurp yours!

THE COMTE D'ARTOIS
(in a fine state due to the action he has just performed)

You're right; you need a similar argument.

He then exposes to the two ladies' gazes the regenerator of the human race.

THE QUEEN
(eyes aglow, bosom throbbing)

Ah! And what a fine argument! What do you say, Polignac?

POLIGNAC

It would be unjust not to be of the same opinion.

THE COMTE D'ARTOIS
(placing a leg between the Queen's knees)

Allow me to press my argument home.

Duet with dialogue

The Comte d'Artois	The Queen
Forgive my intoxication	No. Let me be, my friend;
I don't want to only half	Gently, you're
Prove my affection.	Hurting me.

THE QUEEN

Get a grip on your desire,
When by luck we're brought together
Let's drown together
In waves of pleasure.

THE QUEEN

That's good.

D'ARTOIS

Oh wait...

THE QUEEN

Faster...
What a delicious moment!

D'ARTOIS

Ah! The way you move!
What blissful bucking!

THE QUEEN

Ah! Ah! That's so goooood... I'm coming!

D'ARTOIS

Prepare to receive my soul.

Together
In this moment full of sweet joy, let's drain the cup of happiness.

There is a moment of silence while Mme de Polignac contemplates the happy couple, then says:

POLIGNAC

You've left me high and dry! Happily, while you were so busy, I held *Histoire de Dom Bougre, portier des Chartreux* in one hand, and my other hand wasn't idle.

THE QUEEN
(to the Comte d'Artois)

Oh my dear count, your climax is so delicious! You've taken me out of myself...I am still savoring the pleasure you've just given me to taste.

D'ARTOIS

I hope my Priapus won't stop there. *(The count reveals his still vigorous tool.)* It's ready for another bout, as you can see.

POLIGNAC

The good Monarch is giving you plenty of time; he's snoring like a Templar.

THE QUEEN

Of course! His being sound asleep gives me the wildest idea!

D'ARTOIS

What is it?

THE QUEEN

He must assist our love making. The way he's sitting fits in with my scheme. I can't help laughing already.

D'ARTOIS

Let's do it, now.

THE QUEEN

Oh yes, I can't hold back any longer...Let's sit like this. *(The Queen pulls up two stools on either side of the King's back. Mme de Polignac sits on Louis XVI's back and, parting her legs, places each of her feet on a stool. Antoinette leans forward into Polignac's arms, holding her tight, while her tongue seeks and plays with that of the Confidente. She thereby offers Comte d'Artois the most beautiful rump in the world, saying to him:)*
Well, Count, you can see what route remains for you to take.

D'ARTOIS

And I'll take it without further ado. *(He lifts up a light lawn petticoat, uncovering two buttocks as white as snow; then, furtively opening up with his hand the route to voluptuous pleasure, he launches the arrow of love into the temple of bliss. While the women's tongues are flicking, while supple loins are bucking, seeking new pleasures, the Confidente introduces her little finger into the portico of the Temple into which the Count has introduced himself by a detour.)*

THE QUEEN

The poor old Monarch! I'm sure that if he woke up right now, I could make him believe he's seeing things. It's so easy to get him to believe anything I like. *(To the Comte d'Artois, who's still going full bore:)* Stop for a moment. *(To the Duchess:)* You too, Polignac; let me have a little chuckle over our tableau. This new group should be added to Arétino's studies... Ah! *(Lascivious Antoinette's voice fails her, and a voluptuous silence follows her joke.)*

But a bodyguard who saw everything through the doorway promises himself to stage this proverbial-opera *scene, whose motto will be:*

Dimmi con chi tu vai, e sapero qual che fai.

So he wrote the following quatrain, inspired by the sight of the above scene:

Quatrain

On a human Monarch's back
I see the Mother of Vice
Plunged in fearful pleasures twice
A whorish queen, a princely hack.
A lout of a Prince and a prostitute Queen.

(Bibliothèque Nationale, Rés. 8° L6392401;
Bibliothèque Historique de la Ville de Paris, 611156, 15709;
Bibliothèque de l'Arsenal, Rf 16.147)

BORD...   R.....

*Suivi d'un entretien secret entre la Reine
et le Cardinal de Rohan, après son
entrée aux Etats-généraux.*

Le B. se trouve à Versailles, dans l'appartement de la Reine.

The Royal Bordello

Followed by a Secret Interview
Between the Queen and Cardinal de Rohan
After his Entry into the Estates General

The B[ordello] is located at Versailles,
in the Queen's apartments

The Queen and her Chambermaid

THE QUEEN

At last the moment has come when my mind, fatigued by the rau-
cous cry of the frogs of the Seine, can relax and enjoy at leisure
the pleasures one experiences on Cythera. I thought I was going
to remain a widow since my brother the Comte d'Artois was banished; but no such thing: this evening I shall be visited by the
Knight of B——, the Baron of B——, the Marquis d'H——,
and the Bishop of R——; their presence will console me for a
loss I had thought inconsolable. What do you say, spinner of my
pleasures?

THE CHAMBERMAID

You are easily consoled . . . I'm not like you. Since Polignac's departure, I'm tired of being your pleasure spinner. Even if it means displeasing the frogs of the Seine, I'd like to see the Comte d'Artois and Mme Polignac return ... Then the three of you could spin together.

ANTOINETTE

How very impertinent of you ... but here come Cythera's chimneysweeps. Be good and prepare six bowls of broth, which we will have two hours from now, after I've got them going with smutty talk.

THE CHAMBERMAID

I'll be off ... but take care not to fuck too much. Only put the Bishop of R —— to work — as a fuck he's worth four others.

ANTOINETTE

Don't worry ... six of their kind don't frighten me. Off you go then! Do what I ask ...

Antoinette goes into her apartments, where the above-mentioned persons are. She finds them stark naked, their pistols erect and ready to draw. Carried away with joy, the Queen would like to take her clothes off too. But two knots check her sudden desire to reveal the seat of her virginity, which she lost three years before her marriage; she cuts them with scissors to have done with them the sooner, forgetting that after she's had her pleasure she'll need to attach the petticoat with strings. Her feather brain didn't consider that. She was well and truly caught out, as you will see from the following.

THE KNIGHT OF B ———
(showing his b∗∗∗s and singing the following refrain)

Good evening, my queen,
Regard my charms,
These bells are keen,
You, who keep cocks warm:
If you play these bells,
I'm heard o'er the dells.

ANTOINETTE
(opening the gates to the Temple of Love)

Oh Knight! I won't answer you in poetry. I speak only prose.
You're the only one who can pull off the double feat of being a
fine poet and a fine f∗∗∗. It's not due to the first title that I open
the gates for you, but the second — that you're a good f∗∗∗. I need
that more; come in, the door's open.

THE KNIGHT
(holding his c∗∗∗ in his hand)

Love made a poet of me... You inspired my poem... Ah! Sweet,
happy moment...

*So he lies on top of her... The Baron, the Marquis, and the Bishop
bugger each other while awaiting their turn.*

ANTOINETTE
(addressing the buggers)

Sleazy bawds, how impatient you are! Couldn't you wait till the

219

Knight finished the job? You could have infused your procreative broth in my pot. ⎜

THE BISHOP

There's more where that came from — even more than you need. I've got enough to fill your pot.

THE BARON

No you don't, you rogue; let me contribute my share.

THE MARQUIS

I don't think mine will go astray.

THE QUEEN

You're gallant lads ... clearly ... I see I'm dealing with real blades. Come on then, Knight, hurry up; you've been on me long enough ... It's the Abbot's turn.

THE BARON

I don't consent — and neither should you, Marquis. When that f***er is on the mare, he never gets off.

THE BISHOP

I'm making quite a sacrifice, but still I'll consent to letting you others go first ... I'll make up for lost time once you've f***ed her.

ANTOINETTE

Nice to see you're so reasonable today, Abbot... You can stay as long as you like. Draw your sword, Marquis, shoot; hurry up and f*** me, you've only got a quarter of an hour.*

The quarter of an hour having elapsed, the Baron does likewise. Then it's the Bishop's turn.

THE QUEEN

Abbot, baptize my c***, wipe out the stain of original sin. Nothing is more salutary than this holy water.

THE BISHOP

You're right... Nothing is more salutary than this water. It's like an aqua fortis. It delivers virgins from their virginity, which never returns. It's medicine for the first signs of flu in May. If we sold it by the bottle, what a profit we'd make! But we're silly enough to give it secretly to virgins and those who'd like to pass themselves off as such; we're silly enough, I tell you, to offer them money — and even then we don't get much of a deal.

---

* Such are the familiar expressions of this lascivious woman. We record her conversation word for word, as it actually took place since the arrival of Cardinal de Rohan. The reader will pardon our precision in reporting the facts. We are merely echoing this Messalina.

ANTOINETTE

You can't complain, Abbot; it's not as though you have to fork it out of your own pocket. I've paid you for your water...I had you given a bishoprick for watering my garden ten times, and you've got some nice abbeys on top of that. What more do you want? Take your hose in hand, Abbot, and water my garden.

THE BISHOP

Your garden's like a sponge — worse than a sponge, for as soon as a sponge has all the water it can take, it stops drinking. Your garden, on the contrary, no matter how often watered, never gets wet enough. It's dry as soon as it's soaked. I know...your garden lies on the equator: it's very hot there.

ANTOINETTE

So what? That's how I am. My garden needs frequent watering. Otherwise it would soon become a dried out crust. So get on with it...I'm burning...

The Bishop lies on top of her and stays there for half an hour.

THE KNIGHT

Hurry up, Abbot, you're taking your time. All these scoundrels are the same: once they're in the citadel of Cythera, they don't ever want to pull out. Out you come, you lout, you're wearing our obliging Lydia out.

ANTOINETTE

Hear that, cunt-grip? Get off now. It's time for soup; we've had enough bawdiness. I'll call my chambermaid.

(She immediately pulls the bell, the Abbot gets down, the Chamber-maid brings in five bowls of broth.)

THE CHAMBERMAID

Here, my bawds, a little restorative. You need it. *(They each take a bowl.) (The Chambermaid, addressing the Queen:)* Madame, can you give Cardinal de Rohan a hearing? He has come to pay you his respects. Shall I let him in?

ANTOINETTE

Yes, I'd like to appear to reconcile myself with him ... He has yet to fall for any of the traps I've set him, so it's in my interest to be nice to him. That way I'll make him forget all the wrongs I've done him. As for you, my friends, go quietly into the other room; it has beds. You've had your fun, now rest; don't make a sound.

They leave. The Queen immediately grabs her petticoat. At that moment, Cardinal de Rohan enters.

THE QUEEN

Ah, there you are, Cardinal! Please excuse me. I haven't put my petticoat on yet. The ribbons have snapped. My dear Cardinal, I'd be very grateful if you'd help me do them up again.

THE CARDINAL

With great pleasure.

Immediately undertaking the task, he puts her petticoat on and slips his hand underneath it. Not in her pocket but...

ANTOINETTE

I'm very pleased, Cardinal, to see you in the Estates General.* I do hope you won't be cross with me any more. I'm truly sorry to have been the cause of your disgrace.

THE CARDINAL

I forgive you from the bottom of my heart. But allow me to make a few small observations. Since I've known you for four years, it's time I opened my heart to you and asked you why you hate me.

---

* It seems that falseness is hereditary in the House of Austria. All the Courts of Europe distrust the Court of Vienna. She brought it as dowry to our good King Louis XVI. Consider her falseness in conversation. A tigress whose little ones had been taken from her could not have been more ferocious to the ravisher than she was to Cardinal de Rohan. Although her feelings about him hadn't changed, she pretends to be nice to him. The judicious reader can easily guess the reason.

ANTOINETTE

I didn't want to talk about it further. I'd have preferred it had you forgotten all about the matter. But since you ask, I'll make it brief. Do you remember that night, when I asked you to come and sleep with me, and you said you'd be over? You failed to keep your word. I learned that you were at Lamotte's. [*sic*] I was so stung by such idiocy that I swore eternal hatred for you. But I've forgotten. Let's live on good terms from now on.

THE CARDINAL

I remember well. I wasn't to blame. You wanted me to come and sleep with you. But I had already caressed you four times that day. I needed a rest. Shouldn't you have shown more consideration for the father of the Dauphin and perhaps the Dauphine?

THE QUEEN

All right, my mistake. Let's make peace. Let's forget the past. You will always be my Husband. I'll do all I can to reconcile you with the King.

THE CARDINAL

That's all very well, but you can never get me back my office of Grand Chaplain. Cardinal de Montmorency isn't inclined to resign.

THE QUEEN

Don't worry. I promise you you'll get it back. Just as I had the power to remove you from it, so can I remove the Bishop of Metz. With that in mind, I'll go and butter up the King; I'll make him swig down two good bottles of wine. That way I can get him to agree to anything. *(The Queen puts her arms around his neck.)* So, my dear Cardinal, forget all the nasty things I've done to you. I'll soon be announcing your possession of the office of Grand Chaplaincy. Meanwhile, I have a favor to ask of you: In Paris they're publishing my life story, the memoirs of the comtesse de Lamotte. Have all copies remanded; bring every one of them to me.

THE CARDINAL

That can't be done. Nearly everyone in Paris has a copy at home. Say nothing. Take heart. Your Frenchman easily shakes off his impressions. I have one piece of advice to give you: if you wish to regain his friendship, make him generous gifts. Pray to God morning and night. Do it in such a way that the public learns of it. I promise you they will adore you as much as they deride you now.

THE QUEEN

I'll take your advice, starting from today. When you want to be naughty, come here in secret. No one will know a thing. I'll play the devout soul.

THE CARDINAL

You'd do well to. Tonight I'll come and sleep with you. I'll get one of my servants to dress up as the Cardinal, and send him to my mansion in Paris. They'll think it's me. Tonight we'll work on a new Duke of Normandy. I'll go now and return this evening.

THE QUEEN

Agreed. I'll be waiting for you.

(Bibliothèque Nationale, Enfer 605, variant Enfer 606)

L A
LIGUE ARISTOCRATIQUE

O U

LES CATILINAIRES FRANÇOISES,

PAR un Membre du Comité Patriotique du
Caveau.

Illuſtres Scélérats, Patricides pervers,
Je veux de vos forfaits inſtruire l'Univers.

AU PALAIS-ROYAL,

De l'Imprimerie de JOSSERAN, Auteur des
Motions nouvelles.

---

1 7 8 9.

The Aristocratic League,
or The French Catalinas[1]

By a Member of the Patriotic Committee of the Vault

Renowned Villains, Perverse Patricides,
Let me tell the Universe of your Criminal Deeds.

THE PALAIS-ROYAL
From the Press of JOSSERAN,
Author of New Motions
1789

Vile Courtesans crowned by a Fury, criminal accomplices of a sacrilegious rebel, dangerous subjects of the best of Kings, and pernicious Citizens of the most powerful of Empires, it is time to reveal your seditious plots against the Nation, and to ban your odious names throughout the Universe.

Yes, it is you, dissolute Prince, unnatural Brother, it is your fiery spirit, it is your vicious soul, that stirs up sedition, and breathes hatred.

It is in the boudoirs of a Messalina,* that, seated on sofas soiled by criminal acts, the Peers of the Realm, Tyrants of Peoples, friends of the Queen, and enemies of the King, swear oaths of conspiracy through the medium of Vermont,† Priest of Crime, and on the breast of la Polignac, Altar of Vice.

It is there that Conti‡ and Condé, deputy leaders of the League, gather around the implacable and lustful Austrian Woman, the cunning Luxembourgs and d'Hénin, the traitor d'Antrague, and the perfidious Despréménil; it is there that the murderous mob of the three Coignys,§ the Duras clan, and the Vintimilles furtively move in a pack; it is there that both the Marquis d'Autichen and the Duc de Guiche degrade and dishonor themselves as they please; it is there that the vile Curalexes, the Guignes, and the Polignacs crawl and slither.

More than twenty other conspirators, introduced by the base valet Thierry, come under cover of darkness to take part in this diabolical Assembly. Their eyes sparkling with rage are the only lights illuminating these sorts of nocturnal sabbaths. The outlaws divide into clusters to deliberate the means of overthrowing their country and their King. On one side are Cossé,

---

* Epithets well earned, after the lewd caresses proffered in her apartments to the dissolute Péguigny, St. Maigrin, Cossé, and Mailly, as well as Guéméné, Polignac, La Motte, etc., and after the lascivious pleasures enjoyed in the gardens with the debauched Dilon, Coigny, Bezenval, Vaudreuil, Campan and Bazin, as well as with the insolent Abbot of Vermont, and the apprentice war clerk, etc.

† The abbé Vermont, corrupter and vile Minister for Pleasure, say *The Historical Essays on the Life of Marie-Antoinette*. See especially note 17.

‡ At the Palais-Royal it was uttered that the Prince de Conti had written to some nobles to hold fast, and that they would find a favorable moment.

§ One of the three is the Father of Madame.

Vaudreuil,* Mailly, Berchigny, and Montagnac, on another, Coilla, Choiseul, Meuse, Serrant, and Vaudemon. Over there Breteuil, Montaigu, Bostel, and Narbonne gather. Here Monthosier, Esmagur, and Martel unite, rebels determined to ravage the Realm, as well as du Châtelet, Broglio, and Bezenval, outlaws ready to set the Capital ablaze.

A Princess and two Countesses, or rather three furies, going under the names of Monaco, de Lamberty, and d'Autichien, go from one cluster to the next, shaking their torches and coaxing their hissing serpents to fan the flames of these abhorrent plots.

In addition, certain Cabalists say, these Demoniacs, in amassing scores of evil deeds, invoke infernal powers, raise Altars to them and to them pray, and make sacrifices and sacrilegious offerings to obtain the destruction of the Empire. They also say that, thanks to these superstitious practices, their party has swollen to over eight hundred secret conspirators.†

What else do these unbridled Henchmen of the raging Female Sovereign do? After forming a league with the Ministers, to buy influence and sell favors, after casting aside their Nobility in calculated alliances with those of ignoble birth; after having united Bellona's scepter with Mercury's wand; after having corrupted our Magistrates with the gold of Croesus and Phrynise's bosom; after having had the Tribunals shut down to deprive us of distributive justice, they turn our Archons into chiefs of sedition;‡ they form leagues with the Pontiffs of Religion, and have them brazenly raise the standard of revolt.

---

* This is the father of the Dauphin. La Polignac, during a confinement, lent him to the Queen, as a producer of boys. That's the kind of woman she is.

† One knows what superstition made Priests do at Mass, in the days of the League.

‡ All these facts are so well known, they no longer require proof.

Yes, Monsters, your sordid and murderous confederation goes even further: it seizes all our grains and grinds them with poison, forcing us to buy death while overcharging us for life.* You were the driving force, the accomplices of the execrable Foulon and the odious Sauvigny; like them you deserve to have your corrupt hearts ripped out and to have dragged through the mire your venomous bodies which you've already steeped in vice.

I come back to you, Princes to the King, you infamous nobles and regicidal Triumvirs; I openly denounce the hideous scheme you hatched to tear down virtue's shield by dividing Necker from Louis;† to have the Deputies of the Third Estate's throats cut; and to reenact (on St. Peter's Day) the St. Bartholomew's Day Massacre.

Indeed, that is what would have happened, if the loyal Helvetian troups had obeyed the orders of their fiery Colonel.‡ At that moment a thousand ready torches would have set the Palace of our Kings ablaze; their worthy heir would have perished in the flames, and Paris would now be a second Troy; rivers of blood would have inundated France; the usurpers' Henchmen would have slit the People's throats; but the spirits of their victims would have returned once more to demand their master.

Marvelous! One of you wished to appear virtuous; he feigned love for his King. For the rest of you such an effort will be

---

* Recently it was a proverb in Paris that wheat sacks were tied with red and blue ropes.

† One scarcely dares recall the scurrilous action and the cruel threat made by the comte d'Artois to M. Necker, to force him to leave the Ministry; it is consigned to other works.

‡ During the riot following the dismissal of M. Necker, on June 24, on which occasion M. d'Artois commanded the Swiss to draw on the People, which they wisely refused to do.

suspect; we will scrutinise his heart, we will light up that muddy labyrinth, and we will see if a man long enervated by the most vile pleasures of vice can tolerate the great impulses of virtue.

Illustrious villains, your plans were forestalled, but your rage was not appeased. Six of your men who ravaged the countryside drove fifty thousand assassins and a hundred thunderbolts of war, all dedicated to cutting our Citizens' throats and setting our Capital on fire overnight. Already six thousand Germanic brigands set out ahead of them to ravage her. Already Lambesc, more fiery than the steed bearing him, heads full pelt for the gardens of our Kings, and dares there crush the crowd — striking, bowling over, knocking down — women, children, and the elderly.*

But God exhales; and the schemes of the evil are blown away. On the same day we unhatch all their plots; our bourgeois communities transform themselves into legions of warriors; we exterminate their brigands; we seize hold of their arms, their supplies, their rations. Nothing can resist us; we force the doors of the Invalides, the Bastille falls under our blows; we immolate two traitors, and thanks to a valor that the Romans would have envied us, and to exploits posterity may doubt, the day† the traitors had marked for the ruin of our Empire was the moment both of its liberation and its triumph.

Proud of the valor of my Compatriots, seated on the trophies of their glory, the rubble of the Bastille, trampling underfoot its overturned towers, I am not afraid of publishing the secret crimes of hatred. Yes, it is hatred that covers its rage with the mask of gaiety; it is hatred that, in a nocturnal orgy,‡ fully engaged in the

---

* The old man accused of murder was badly hurt, but did not die.

† July 14, 1789.

‡ The ball mentioned in the sequel to *Le Point du jour*, and in *Les Nouvelles Philippiques*,[2] etc.

scheme of our destruction, and transported by mystical sounds, gives itself over to the most lascivious dancing; it is hatred again that offers itself up to the two Venuses, makes sacrifices to Love and libations to Priapus, along with the Energumenes, whom hatred enlists under its bloody flags; it is hatred that, having transformed its daggers into pistols,* hid one in its bosom with which to assassinate the liberator of the Monarch and the Nation. It is hatred that is transforming all the country houses of our Princes into so many rebel arsenals; it is hatred that bribes, drives, directs the villains to make away daily with our powder and our ammunition. It is hatred that makes them pass around a great many uniforms similar to our own, the better to disguise their treachery;† hatred that makes those combustible dragnets that one finds stored in our cellars,‡ new sorts of mines invented to blow our houses to bits. It is hatred that stirs up all the daily factions in our provinces. Hatred it is that dreamed up, and Montaigu who executed, the odious and diabolical scheme of mining the castle of

* Several persons attest that on Friday, July 17, the duc d'Orléans, having been to the King's early in the morning to persuade him to go to Paris to calm the People, and thereby regain his realm, Thierry de Villedavrai, his valet, went and begged the Prince to go to the Queen's. H.M., on the point of leaving, also wished to go and see her. Antoinette, outraged at seeing her enemy with company, fainted at the sight of her husband; and as they were undoing her stays, a pistol fell from her breast.

† On Tuesday, August 12, three large boats were seized on which there were at least twenty thousand uniforms of the Royal Grenadiers.

‡ On Saturday, August 8, in the streets of Paris, baskets were found filled with strips of cloth coated with sulphur, and after thorough searching, several pieces were found thrown in different cellars, among others that of a carpenter, in the rue St. Bon.

Guincé, giving a ball* there and then igniting a thunderous, infernal explosion, which buried thousands of guests beneath a heap of rubble.

What apart from implacable hatred could have persuaded a brother, who was already incestuous, to become fratricidal? This he would have become, though, one night — one terrible night! — if Destaing, ever faithful to his Kings, and faithful to his Country, hadn't uncovered the mysterious plot and prevented its bloody execution. Thrice villain! To desire to kill a brother! a friend! a King! May you wander the earth, if you dare, and drag out a miserable life from climate to climate; may you be chased from Courts and hated by Peoples.† May you expire in the torment of remorse. And lastly, may the last of your nephews still curse your memory.

My mind stunned, my heart seized by such wicked deeds, I can no longer describe them... But what's this I hear? In our provinces we read a pathetic, touching letter from the unfortunate children of these renowned outlaws. These hapless little things protest their innocence and beg pardon for themselves... Ah poor victims! We can only pity you, we dare not acknowledge you. The authors of your existence are the cause of your ruin. It is almost a crime to owe one's birth to them. The blood of the smallest serpents still produces vipers. Renounce this nobility that degrades virtue; flee the lands where your fathers enjoyed it! Go and take shelter under the most obscure names; forget on Shepherds' stools that you could mount the throne of Kings.

* Ball given on July 19, 1789 by Mesmai de Montaigu, Counsellor at the *parlement* of Besançon, in the gardens of his castle at Guincé, in the Vezoul, Franche-Comté.

† The three fugitive Princes, on arriving in Brussels, were spurned by the spectators of the Comédie.

As for you, banished Princes, fugitive criminals; as for you, debased Noblemen, rebellious Citizens, I do violence to the hatred that you inspire, and I declare unto you, in the name of the Nation, your Mother, and your Sovereign that we forbid you, as your Fathers, the tyrannical right to subject us to feudal rents. Content yourselves with your dusty titles; be Noblemen, we won't be jealous of you; we are honest folk, and that is more than I can say for you. Administer our armies; bridle our soldiers, command them to valor — that is quite enough for cowards.

I say unto you that if you do not renounce your futile subterfuges, your refuted claims,* your criminal schemes; if you do not hurry up and join, completely, and wholeheartedly, a Nation that you have dishonored by your vices, we will ban your names in the National Senate, and we will work without you and without your corrupt Pontiffs;† under the wing of virtue, before the eyes of LOUIS, and in emulation of his only friend at court, the foreign Patriot, we will work for the regeneration of Our Native Land, for the destruction of Vice, and for the good of the Sovereign.

(Bibliothèque Historique de la Ville de Paris)

---

* On June 30, 1789, the comte d'Ambly, Deputy of the Bailiff's Court of Reims, swears on his honor that his constituents had coerced him into voting only by their order. M. de Sillery, of the same Bailiff's Court, gives him the lie and proves the contrary by quoting items from their records. See *The News from Versailles*, rue du Hurpois, no. 24.

† These really are INTRUDERS, as pernicious to the political order as to the social order, etc., etc., and a thousand times more, etc.

NOTES

1. Lucius Sergius Catilina was an unscrupulous Roman conspirator who was exposed and defeated by Cicero.

2. *Le Point du jour* was a daily newspaper that appeared from June 19, 1789 to October 1, 1791. *Les Nouvelles Philippiques* is the title of a pamphlet.

DESCRIPTION

DE LA

MENAGERIE ROYALE

D'ANIMAUX VIVANS,

ÉTABLIE AUX THUILERIES,

PRÈS DE LA TERRASSE NATIONALE,

Avec leurs noms, qualités, couleurs et propriétés.

Il y a depuis quelque tems dans le château de Henri IV, une ménagerie véritablement curieuse, tant par la rareté des animaux qui la composent, que par la dépense excessive que son entretien coûte à la nation.

Le public a examiné les bêtes féroces qui étaient dans leurs cages respectives, dans le parc de Versailles ; il peut voir plus commodément et sans se déranger beaucoup, une quantité de quadrupèdes rassemblés au Louvre. Nous allons citer les plus remarquables de ces bêtes féroces ; indiquer leurs habitudes et leurs inclination ; leur manière de se nourir, et leurs propriétés.

Description

of the Royal Menagerie

# of Living Animals

Established in the Tuileries
Near the National Terrace

With their names, features,
colors, and characteristics

For some time now in Henri IV's castle there has been a truly curious zoo — curious as much for the rarity of the animals in it, as for the excessive expenditure that its maintenance costs the nation.

The public has inspected the ferocious beasts in their respective cages in the park at Versailles; they can watch more comfortably, and without going to much trouble, a number of quadrupeds gathered at the Louvre. We will list the most remarkable of these ferocious beasts, note their habits and their inclinations, their manner of feeding and other characteristics.

I. The Royal Veto
This animal is about five feet, five inches long. He walks on his hind legs the way men do. The color of his fur is tawny. He

has dull eyes, a fairly wide gob, a red muzzle, and big ears; not much of a mane; his cry rather resembles the grunt of a pig; HE DOESN'T HAVE A TAIL.

He is voracious by nature; he eats, or rather, sloppily devours, anything one throws at him. He is a drunk and never stops drinking, from first thing in the morning to last thing at night.

The Royal Veto is as timid as a mouse, and as stupid as an ostrich; he is in fact a fat animal, which, it would seem, nature was sorry to have created.

His food costs about twenty-five to thirty million a year. And he is not grateful either; on the contrary, he seeks only to do harm, and his cunning and vulgar spirit often propels him against the walls of the national terrace, where he sometimes breaks his nose.

He is thirty-four to thirty-six years old. He was born at Versailles and given the nickname "Louis XVI."

II. *The Female Royal Veto*

The female of the Royal Veto is a monster found in Vienna, Austria, in the wardrobe of the empress, Maria Theresa. This crowned she-ape probably felt an unnatural urge: no doubt she had herself bedded by a tiger or a bear and brought MARIE-ANTOINETTE into the world.

This monster, aged thirty-three, was brought to France in the days of the incestuous Louis XV, whose memory is odious. As she combined the falseness of her country with the natural perfidiousness of beasts who wear tiaras, she at first presented herself to the people as angelically sweet. They cried: LONG LIVE THE QUEEN! Now, once she was assured that she could acknowledge the ninnies' allegiance with a few grimaces, she took off her mask and became known for what she really was.

Married for political reasons to a zombie who spends his time making locks and bolts, like Dion of Syracuse, she soon cooked up ways of amusing herself at the expense of all and sundry. All one ever heard talk of then was the Parc-aux-Cerfs, Bagatelle, Trianon, the *Décampativos*, and famous gatherings of people from the four corners of the earth, in which the Royal Veto was always the chamber pot; one only ever heard talk of the d'Artoises and the female Polignacs, the Vaudreuils and bodyguards, the King and his concierge, the Cardinal and Cagliostro, the diamond necklace and the unfortunate d'Oliva, who died of poison. The Heavens spurned the abominations and crimes of the Austrian Woman, the Austrian Woman mocked the Heavens and the nation: the people rise up, and lo and behold, the Siren from Austria takes a child in her arms (this was the dauphin); she escapes through the same hands she would like to have seen in fetters. Now you have the Versailles zoo transferred to Paris... Now you have the female of the Royal Veto conjuring up, with an animal called Lafayette, a little trip to the border; now you have the chameleon passing herself off as the Baroness de Korff, with Louis XVI, King of France, her manservant, and he would have been made to sit behind the carriage too, if some other male had been rutting... Now you have the gang stopped and driven back to Paris, where intrigues are well under way, and this is how Marie-Antoinette of Austria entertains herself by disturbing the peace of free France.

Recently a prostitute was condemned to six months' imprisonment for having insulted a citizen... If Marie-Antoinette were to be judged as she deserves... she would be in good company in the Salpêtrière.

The female of the Royal Veto is lanky, ugly, wrinkled, worn-out, faded, hideous, frightful; but since the nation is stupid enough to feed its tyrants, she eats France's money in the hope of one day devouring the French, one by one.

III. The Delphinus

We will say nothing about the Delphinus. We have noticed that there is sometimes a young shoot on a rotten tree... Whose son is the Delphinus? Let's hope he doesn't wind up poisoned like his unfortunate brother!

IV. The Royal Madame

This little female, no doubt designed, like the spiders of the French Cape, to suck the blood of slaves, already has all her mother's haughtiness and perhaps her vices as well. It wouldn't hurt if she were trained in a trade of some kind; instead of queen, she could well be a darner of stockings one day.

V. The Elisabeth Veto

The sister of the Royal Veto is as nasty as she once was pretty. This evil slut would like to see the nation go to the dogs; but she has a share in the tyrant's food allowance and she earns her keep well... Who does keep her?

VI. The Royal Veto Provence

All that is most cunning and shrewd in the fox is to be found multiplied by the thousand in the innermost recesses of the heart of the Royal Veto Provence.

This hypocritical monster, on learning that Favras had compromised him, waits for the poor man to expire before going in pomp to the Hôtel de Ville, his tail between his legs, to assure his fellow citizens of his attachment to the Constitution; then, lo and behold, he suddenly departs for Koblenz, without paying his debts, and tries to stir up that country's wolf cubs against us.

We are not yet finished with this creature.

The Royal Veto Provence is a fat idiot like his elder brother; he looks black and treacherous... The Bourbon race doubtless resemble the descendants of Cain, bearing on their muzzle the mark of their reprobation and infamy. We will say nothing about his habits. He once used to amuse himself by biting his fingernails; one day he may well bite his fingers for having ingratiated himself with our traitors, among whom he couldn't fail to shine through his evil deeds. But if, having escaped from the royal menagerie, this animal is ever caught... watch out for LOUISE.*

VII. The Royal Veto d'Artois

Resembling the venomous asp, only lively and of slight build, the Royal Veto d'Artois is perhaps the prettiest beast of all the royal menagerie, but not the least vicious.

An animal without morals, having the lasciviousness of a wild boar,† the lewdness of Louis XV, the debauched dissoluteness characteristic of the louts of the court, d'Artois, before the revolution, displayed only vice and a heart made for crime; all he lacked to be covered in glory was a counterrevolution; but what horrors were to go before!

The steamy ANTOINETTE, that same female of the ROYAL VETO, was not indifferent to him. He found that she was worth the trouble... Bagatelle, Trianon, Meudon, copses and caverns resounded to the sound of their erotic spasms... D'Artois flew into the arms of girls with tiaras or the wrong kind of petticoat. It was all the same to him. Dissolute lecher, bereft of faith, honor, and God — here you have another of those animals who think that all they have to do is act, waiving all principles, and they'll succeed in getting a people born for liberty to crawl under their iron rod! We will shortly return to the subject of this ferocious

*The little machine that cuts off heads so nicely.
† Male pig.

243

beast; we will not forget the bragging and boasting of that other fugitive animal known as Condé. Let us examine briefly our enemies' conduct. Let us no longer entertain ourselves by making futile reproaches. It is in hand combat that we should wage war against them to the death. It is important for us, it is important for the children of liberty to show the supporters of slavery that nothing can shake us.

Less outraged by the boasting of Prussia or Hungary than filled with the deepest contempt for speculators in our war, we will indignantly reject the perfidious advice that the courts of France, Berlin, and Vienna give us.

Indeed, show me the sane man who would prefer the old order to the new ... even allowing that the current order of things cannot go on. You see how the treacherous Louis XVI is unworthy of ruling over you.

I can prove what I am putting forward: either Louis XVI is an aristocrat or he is a patriot.

If he is an aristocrat, I ask any antirevolutionary if he does not find, in Louis XVI, a shabby party chief. Has not the apparent wrong done to the aristocrats by the King remained in their souls? Can they see a protector in Louis XVI? Does he arm himself with daggers? They are kicked in the arse in front of him ... When they try to drag him to Montméry, they are confounded, and Louis XVI plays into the others' hands. Now there's a well-founded love for a faithless king for you! Poor Louis XVI, can you not see that if the aristocrats live and breathe the ancien régime alone, if they want to restore the nobility and the monasteries, it would only be to dethrone you and lock you away in a cloister? There, with your head shaved and dressed in a long monk's frock, reduced to a mean existence, you would be perfectly certain of the eternal scorn of those whom your wife calls her dear gentlemen and her holy fathers.

I would now like to know in what Louis XVI's patriotism consists.

Answer us, Marie-Antoinette: what have you done with your husband's heart? You have weakened your spouse, you have cunningly brutalized him. One could not speak to his majesty because HIS MAJESTY WAS DRUNK. One could not speak to his majesty, HE WAS MAKING LOCKS. One could not speak to his majesty, HE WAS OUT HUNTING.

And you, flitting from one pleasure to the next, from one intrigue to the next, you reigned in his name, you were everything in his name.

What baseness and arrogance, what boldness and duplicity, what protests of public-spiritedness and underhanded plots!

Perverted mother, you abandon your son on his death bed! Oh, you know only too well who pushed him into the grave! His last words denounce you. He said to his governor, "Take this lock of my hair to my mother, so that she will remember me..." Answer, cruel mother!...He is dead!...

Wife with no sense of decency, you prostitute yourself to fearful pleasures...Born to become the most contemptible of courtesans, the only trace you have of royalty is the impudence; of maternity, the name; of modesty, nothing, not even the appearance; of frankness, no knowledge; of virtue, no experience.

Monster in every way, one cannot look at you without trembling or imagine you without thinking of Jezebel...There is no Jehovah to sacrifice you to, we despise you too much...but there are dogs to feast on your corpse...They are waiting for you...

Presently, imperious creature, you will want to ape Semiramis ...It is true you have not yet killed your husband, but was it not just this action that you sought to commit at Versailles, during your departure for Montméry, baronne de Korff? You made a manservant of your king!

You come with your son in your arms to tell us that you will bring him up according to the constitution!

The constitution of Koblenz, no doubt...

You graciously welcome the National Guard — you would like to bathe in its blood.

You have ruined your husband... You have torn from him the heart of the French people; you have sacrificed him to your pride, to your d'Artois!

Thousands and thousands of plots are hatched before your eyes... You weave them all!...

Antoinette!... There is a prison where they lock up bad women...

And you, King without a crown, since you no longer wish to wear it... Stupid, spineless man; let's see, what would you like us to do to you?

Louis... there is still time, you can win back the esteem of the nation, even the love of the French... you have only one means of being sure of succeeding, and that is to hand over the list of all those who have wronged you!... And to abandon your Louvre to the wicked, until they are tossed out of it!... Then you might be happy... everything would be all right... but there is no going back... or you will be dethroned.

F. DANTALLE

From the PATRIOTS Press

(Bibliothèque Nationale, 8°L6396056;
Bibliothèque Historique de la Ville de Paris,
8641, 955952, 600509, 15520 [nog])

TESTAMENT

DE

MARIE ANTOINETTE,

VEUVE CAPET;

Et détail de tous les circonstances et particularités
qui ont précédées, accompagnées et suivies l'exé-
cution de cette femme abominable.

Peuple! que ton pouvoir est grand et redoutable!
Qui pourra se cacher au trait inévitable,
Dont tu poursuis l'impie au jour de ta fureur!
A punir les méchans ta colere fidele,
  Fait marcher devant elle
  La mort et la terreur.

HOMMES Français, Peuple Républicain, que
le monde te donne le salut fraternel, que l'hu-
manité entière élève vers toi le cri de la recon-
noissance; tu as purgée la terre d'un monstre qui
en étoit l'horreur! Cette femme exécrable que
l'odieuse maison d'Autriche avoit envoyée parmi
nous pour satisfaire sa haine, sa soif ambitieuse &

The Testament of

Marie-Antoinette,

the Widow Capet

With details of all the
circumstances and particularities that have
preceded, accompanied, and
followed the execution of this
abominable woman

People, how great and fearsome is your power!
Who could hide from the ineluctable arrow
With which you pursue blasphemers on the day of fury?
In punishing the wicked your faithful anger
      Makes death and terror
      March before it.

Frenchmen, Republicans, may the world give you the fraternal
nod, may the whole of humanity raise up its voice to you in a cry
of gratitude. You have purged the earth of a monster who was its
abomination! That loathsome woman, whom the odious House of
Austria sent among us to gratify its hatred and its ambitious thirst
and to plunge us into an abyss of calamity, that infernal Fury who
only asked to bathe in French blood, Antoinette, in short, that
Messalina without shame, that new Fredegond; by a dire act of
capital punishment, you have just sent her hurtling into the night
of death. You have forced her to expiate on the scaffold her long
outrages against your sovereignty, her squandering, her cruelties,

and the scandal that her corruption and her unbridled debauchery caused whilever she was alive.

In causing the head of Louis Capet, her *worthy* spouse, to fall, you, the people, had yet only half obtained justice. The Austrian tyrant still flattered itself that it had you sufficiently in its clutches to force you to halt in the middle of your revenge and to become timid when it came to punishing its relative and accomplice. Arrogant and vain hope of a demented despot, to think that when its henchmen had triumphed over our invincible Republicans, we would be cowardly enough to abase ourselves by claiming credit for having saved Antoinette, and that we would be more than happy to accept a shameful peace by handing her over. But how little able is the mind and heart of a tyrant to conceive the strong, proud, great, and just character of true Republicans, to imagine them capable for a moment of compromising principles, of pausing at whatever consideration before adopting the firm and impassive march of justice! All the powers of the Universe united could not have managed to save the widow of the last tyrant of the French, because she was guilty. For a people like the regenerated Frenchman, the law is stronger than all the worlds revolving in space put together.

Now, show me the man, even the most fanatical royalist, who would dare deny that justice and the law were compelled to deliver the judgment brought against Antoinette? Has it not been established and proven that it is she who has ruined our finances, by handing over to her brother all state revenue, the fruits of the sweat of the poor, so that this tyrant could pay the armies he destined to wage war against us, and so that we would have no further means of resisting him? Has it not been established and proven that it is she who never ceased to advise her husband and to push him headlong into the vast morass of betrayals of which we have been the victims? Has it not been proven that it is she who sought to starve the people through the bread shortage, by storing up our grain or having it buried? Has it not been proven that it is she who was behind all the conspiracies against liberty, who incited and bribed the counterrevolutionary lampoonists, the spies, the murderers of patriots; who propped up the anticivic organizations and gatherings of conspirators; who, in short, heaped plot upon plot to destroy France forever?

Has it not been proven that it is she who was the perpetrator of Louis Capet's protests against the Constitution, and his flight to Varennes? Has it not been proven that it was she who from the beginning governed the plots of the traitor Lafayette and the renegades of the Constituent Assembly? Has it not been proven that the massacre of the Champ-de-Mars, and that of Nancy which preceded it, were her doing? Has it not been proven that it is she who stirred her husband into having the French people butchered on August 10, 1792, and who planned the whole day; who, in fact, decided the fate of the people? — which was very different from what the conspirators had hoped for (they threw down this monster and her husband from the pinnacle of their usurped power, and, once and for all, destroyed the realm of the Feuillants).

No, no one can deny that these crimes have been proven with the most minute evidence. Would we have been republicans then if we had shown the least indulgence for a criminal so atrocious, if the concerns of a feeble policy had been able to stifle the voice of justice? What would the nations for whom we wish to serve as models have said of us? Would they not have been justified in saying that, like those sacerdotal charlatans who preached renunciation of all worldly goods while they were rolling in wealth and stuffing themselves with sensual pleasures and delights, we seek to propagate principles that we do not practice; that we never cease praising the charms of equality, while sparing a guilty woman whom the sword of vengeance lays claim to, and that we would save her from the capital punishment she deserves because she is the aunt of a man who calls himself *king*. Yes, citizens, nations, posterity itself would have the right to thus reproach us, and, from then on, all hope of regenerating humankind would have been lost to us. But you considered all this, and even if the firm march of justice had not been commanded, in the circumstances, on the basis of your principles alone, these reflections would have urged you to take it up.

In another respect, if the peoples whom priests and tyrants still keep in ignorance and slavery understood what a service you have rendered them in chopping off Antoinette's head, how much gratitude would they bestow upon you! Is it not this destructive Fury who had war declared? Is it not she who is the cause of all Europe's being in flames? For two years, millions of men have had their throats cut because there was in France an evil woman for whom the vapor given off by human blood when it is spilled in great floods was a delectable perfume.

Let us now provide the reader with details of the circumstances that preceded and accompanied the punishment of this woman in whom all the French saw, so justly, their most implacable enemy.

During her interrogation, she never ceased to display the brazenness of deep-rooted crime. Her answers were all in the negative. Simon, to whom her son had been entrusted, when called as a witness, reproached her with the impure habits she had imparted to her son, habits that tended only to sew in him the seeds of debauchery and to make his morals as loose as those of his mother. *This is too far beneath my contempt for me to reply*, she answered.

Bailly and Manuel greatly disturbed her with their depositions. With her unofficial defense counsel, she continued to show the greatest duplicity. She let herself slip just once, after having asked Chaveau de La Garde, one of her counsel, if there was juridical proof against her. When he answered that there was none as yet, she said, *In that case, the only thing I am afraid of is Manuel.*

When she was on the stool, people in the courtroom several times expressed the desire to have her stand up so that they could see her better. Pride got the better of her, and she cried out in a kind of fit of rage, *Won't the people soon tire of my fatigue?*

Her arrogant look, when the list of all her crimes should have given her, by devouring her with remorse, a countenance of humility and repentance, often caused those present at her interrogation to murmur. Several times women could not help but call out, *Look how proud she still is.* These words, which Antoinette heard, caused her to say to Chaveau de La Garde, *Was I too dignified in my replies? The people seemed to me to be unhappy with them.*

She handed over to Tronçon Ducondray, her other defense counsel, two gold rings and a lock of hair, for a so-called *Mademoiselle* Jari, residing at the home of a *Madame* La Porte in Yvry. The gift was handed over to the Committee for General Security and, no doubt, the committee checked on this *Demoiselle* Jari to find out why she was so dear to Antoinette.

When her sentence was read to her, the president of the Revolutionary Tribunal asked her if she had any objection to make. *I have none*, she replied. And when she was sent back to the court chamber, she got down from the bench with bravado, opened the balustrade herself, and did not seem in the least affected.

When the time came to conduct her to the scaffold, she asked to go by coach. This distinction, being contrary to the principles of equality, was refused. She then asked to have at least her head covered by a veil, which was also refused.

At four-thirty in the morning, the day before last, the twenty-fifth day of the first month, the Revolutionary Tribunal concluded her trial by reading her sentence. She left the Conciergerie at eleven-thirty and was hauled to the scaffold in the same cart as the other persons condemned to death. She was dressed in a simple white wrap, and on her head she wore a bonnet with a black ribbon. Her face was downcast and very pale, owing to a period she had had in prison, rather than the prospect of the just punishment she was about to suffer; for, right up until her execution, she maintained the bearing and proud, haughty air that are typical of her. She calmly surveyed a numberless people whose cries of *Vive la République!* made the air ring.

Having reached the place de la Révolution, she fixed her gaze with some emotion on the Château des Tuileries. An old confessor, keen to preserve till the last the respect priests so naturally have for tyrants, being seated behind her, and not on the same seat, spoke continually to her, but she did not seem to listen to him or even to hear him. When the cart pulled up in front of the scaffold, Antoinette alighted nimbly and swiftly without need of support, even though her hands were tied behind her back; in the same manner, she climbed the fatal ladder with bravura. Without speaking to the people, she acquiesced to the executioner during his preparations. Her execution and what formed its frightful prelude did not last four minutes. The executioner held her head up for the people to see, to the repeated cheers of *Vive la liberté!*

The moment the executioner tried to strip her of a long handkerchief that she had around her neck, she appeared to endure the operation with difficulty, and she attempted to tug the handkerchief herself, despite having her hands bound. When she fell onto the guillotine block, two medallions attached to her neck with two black ribbons were seen to fall out of her bodice, one representing a portrait of Louis Capet, the other, that of the traitor Lafayette, her agent and favorite in all respects.

One fact which history should set down, and which proves that this abominable woman still had her fanatical followers, is this: as soon as her head fell, a young man forced his way through the guards surrounding the scaffold, threw himself close to the spot where the monster's blood was drenching the ground, and dipped a white handkerchief in it. The violence and the act of this fanatically devoted young henchman made him justly suspect. He was arrested, and on his chest was a medallion painted with a fleur-de-lis and two crossed swords. The people wanted this counterrevolutionary to be executed, then and there, with no further evidence than this proof. Officers from the cavalry and aides-de-camp surrounded him. He asked to be protected from the people's fury and to be put in a safe place. Immediately, a municipal officer spoke to the people in the name of the law, explaining to them that this young man might have important papers and facts to reveal that would unmask traitors, that it was up to the law to decide his punishment, and that the magistrates would give the citizens a good account of the proceedings. Suddenly, this same people who never cease to be calumnied, once again gave the lie to their vile detractors. Yielding to the wise words of their magistrate, they cried out, *Yes! Yes!* and formed two rows to allow the fanatical young conspirator to pass. He was conducted by a very small number of guards amid two hundred thousand men who respected their magistrate and the law.

Those are the details surrounding the last moments of the woman whom France in its entirety will always abhor. This is the only testament that she made. The woman who trampled the unhappy people underfoot, who reveled in wealth and pleasure, could only leave, as sole and unique legacy, two gold rings and a lock of her hair. Tyrants! Let this example of the instability of human affairs serve as a lesson to you. Let it be a warning to you of the fate that threatens you. *Vive la République!*

From the press of the Veritable Creole Patriot,
rue Transnonain, former convent of the Carmelites
(Bibliothèque Historique de la Ville de Paris, BHUP 8141)

Designed by Bruce Mau with Barr Gilmore

Printed and casebound by Maple-Vail on Sebago acid-free paper